AWAKENING SOUL FORCE

A Practical Guide to Awakening Truth Within

By Jeff Bomberger

Awakening Soul Force

Copyright © 2019 by Jeff Bomberger

No part of this book may be reproduced without written permission from the publisher or copyright holders, except for a reviewer who may quote brief passages in a review; nor may any part of this book be reproduced, stored in a retrieval system, or transmitted in any form or by any means (electronic, mechanical, photocopying, recording or other) without written permission from the publisher or copyright holders.

Printed by B.C. Allen Publishing and Tonic Books
144 N 7th St. #525
Brooklyn, NY 11249

Now taking manuscript submissions and book ideas at any stage of the process:
submissions@tonicbooks.online

Printed in the United States of America

Cover Design: Teddi Black
Interior Design: Susan Veach

ISBN: 978-1-950977-90-1

5	**Introduction**
17	What Is Soul Force?
27	*Awakening Soul Force* Inspiration
37	The Path Ahead
39	Soul-Force Beginnings
49	Clinging To Truth
53	**Soul-Force Foundations**
61	Conscious Breathing
67	Rhythmic Breathing
73	Soul-Force Field
85	Conscious Release
91	Body Tuning
103	Soul-Force Inventory
135	Everything Is Energy
151	Introduction to Chakras
161	Root Chakra
167	Sacral Chakra
173	Solar Plexus Chakra
179	Heart Chakra
189	Throat Chakra
197	Third-Eye Chakra
207	Crown Chakra
215	Chakra-Balancing Meditation
225	Being Energy Sensitive

235 Soul-Force Reflections

- 237   Deconditioning Thought Experiment
- 243   Mindful Meditation
- 249   Written-Thought Observation
- 257   Witnessing Meditation
- 263   Creative Self-Expression

277 Soul-Force Connection

- 279   Connecting to Soul Force
- 285   Dreaming with Soul Force
- 313   Healing with Soul Force
- 319   Automatic Writing with Soul Force
- 327   We Are Soul Force
- 335   Pledge of Peace, Love, and Unity
- 338   Join the Soul Force

Introduction

You are so much more than you imagine in your human construct. Remember this, and miracles will be made.

A few years ago, I took a shamanic-practitioner workshop through the late Michael Harner's Shamanic Foundation. The workshop was the latest stop on my spiritual journey, where I hoped to explore the philosophy and healing practices of native shamanism more deeply. I'd read a number of books on the subject matter and found that the core tenets of practicing shamanism truly resonated with me. Shamanism is not a religion and requires no religious beliefs; anyone of any faith can practice. As a student of the world's religions and philosophy, I found the inclusivity of this tradition incredibly refreshing. At the heart of shamanism is the idea that spirit permeates all of our universe—everything seen and unseen—and is based on the principle of direct revelation. Direct revelation means that we may access higher wisdom and healing for ourselves and others if we hold a sincere desire to do so. Therefore, shamans, or shamanic practitioners, are people who intentionally work to have direct experience with spirit for the purpose of accessing information, wisdom, and healing for themselves or others.

These concepts were not particularly foreign to me, but I was interested in learning more about the shamanic perspective. When we were kids, my sister and I were briefly brought up in the Catholic faith (I think more out of my mom's sense of obligation to tradition than deep spiritual resonance at that moment in time). My Catholic phase did not last long, but I did find inspiration in the life and teachings of Jesus, and his wisdom remained with me as I turned my young heart toward alternative spiritual horizons. Thanks to my dad, I committed my first real act of religious blasphemy when I received a psychic reading at twelve years old. That reading could very well be considered my first pivotal experience that would shape the trajectory of my spiritual life moving forward. By fifteen, I had made quite a departure from the dogma of the Catholic faith and developed my own meditation practice with the help of psychic John Edward's cassette tape *Unleashing Your Psychic Potential*. Through John's guided meditations, I was exposed to the fundamentals of energy as well as spiritual guidance and energy healing. The knowledge I soaked up from this little cassette tape took root in me in a way that church never had because the information was so practical and personal and the personal impact was so immediate on my young life.

Fast-forward a decade and a half later to a beautiful fall weekend in October. I was now on a five-year stretch of meditating twice a day: once in the morning and once at night. I had a daily visualization routine for protecting my own energy and releasing any negative energy that I might absorb from the day. At least once a week, I was doing chakra work to balance out my spiritual-energy system, and quite regularly I turned to my very active dream life for insights and answers to my own questions about my life and where it was headed. When I felt that magnetic draw I sometimes feel, I would sit down with a pen and a legal pad after a meditation and let words of inspiration flow onto a page. Over the years, I'd come to use this practice to help quell anxious thoughts and help gain clarity when my vision felt clouded. My spiritual practices had grown to be an integral part of my daily life and heavily influenced who I was evolving into as a person. Even with this ongoing spiritual discipline under my belt, nothing could have prepared me for the transformative experience I was about to have "journeying" to the sound of a shamanic drum.

Over the course of the weekend, we performed many intuitive and reflective tasks. We discussed the fundamental ideas guiding shamanic work, including the importance of respecting each and every person's individual spiritual authority. We learned about integrity in the work and the responsibility that comes with working with spirit and energy. We learned about journeying, which is a term used to describe entering an altered state of consciousness to seek the help of spirit. We learned that our intentions must be true when we journey, meaning that we must be sincere and journeying for the highest spiritual growth of ourselves and others. We learned about sonic driving—also known as shamanic drumming—and its role in helping us enter altered states of consciousness. We were shown how to meet our animal guides and work with these helping spirits for the sake of ourselves and others. I was surprised how at home I felt within this work and with these practices.

Finally, one of the more advanced tasks we began working with was performing a shamanic drum journey, with the intention of meeting with a spirit teacher or guide who could provide us with a personal healing. At this particular point in my life, things were running relatively smoothly. I was enjoying two steady contracts as a freelance filmmaker and doing work that was meaningful to me and my community. Even though I was feeling more accomplished in a professional and creative capacity than I had in a long time, instinctively I knew I was still harboring scars in my heart from my failed marriage, which had ended five years earlier. Because part of my own path at this time was learning to more deeply trust my intuition when it spoke, I decided to journey for healing in my heart center. I hoped maybe I could finally shed the hardened scabs still protecting my soft and tender heart. What transpired on this inner journey was nothing short of life altering.

I want to note that this journey was aided only by a simple rhythmic drumbeat. While native traditions have developed a not-so-accurate stereotype of prolifically using psychedelics for healing, there was absolutely no plant medicine involved in our work whatsoever. To me, the results were no less magnificent and humbling. Rather than reconstruct my experience in new language, years removed from the original journey, I'd like to provide a transcription of what I penned immediately after my experience.

I lay down on the cool wood floor of the recreation room we were gathered in. I draped a white bandana over my eyes to prevent any visual distractions from pulling my attention away from the journey. I then began the regular rhythmic breathing I use when entering into a meditative state. After a short initiation with rattles, our facilitator began to hammer away on her shamanic drum. Within moments, my journey began:

> *Started at childhood home, Foreston Drive. Climbed up tree in front yard, all the way up.*

JEFF BOMBERGER

First level pierced a veil above the Earth... I see the Earth's atmosphere.

Bright white—almost sandy desert landscape, but doesn't feel desolate. It's vibrant. A very large Native American Chief dressed in all white: The Guardian of the Heavens. He's not my teacher. I call on Cecil [my animal guide]. He shows up. We go East, get sucked up into a swirling vortex. We jump to level thirteen through this spiraling tunnel.

Land in a beautiful, lush Sequoia-filled forest. A large, blue, giant spirit guide in a winged helmet and armor appears. I ask, "Are you my teacher?" But nothing quite clicks. I ask, "Are you my teacher I am supposed to meet? What's your name?" It's R. Alexander. So I ask Cecil to ask if he's my teacher, and R. Alexander finally says, "I'm your teacher, but not the one you've come to meet." We turn around and go inside the trunk of a big redwood tree, and we go up one more level to level fourteen.

The Council of Masters. GIANTS. IMMENSE. White marble council chamber. Wow.

I am on this rising platform, laid down. They are beaming me up into this beautiful, warm, golden white light, and they work on me... they assemble me.

AWAKENING SOUL FORCE

I ask, "Are you the teachers I am supposed to meet?"

"Yes."

"I am here to heal my heart," I say to them.

They tell me:

"I am John the Baptist. I give you blessings from Heaven." He blesses my body with water.

"I am Persephone. I've given you the ability to see." She touches me in my third eye center.

"I am Maximillian. I've given you a warrior's heart." He touches the center of my chest.

"I am Yashoda. I've given you the healer's touch." She places white light in the center of my palms.

"I am Zephyr. I've given you a voice to communicate." My body trembles with vibration.

I ask, "What does all this have to do with healing my heart?" To which they replied:

"We're showing you who you really are. And who you are cannot be wounded. You are whole. Release the idea that you can be wounded, and you are healed. You are so much more than you imagine in your human construct. Remember this, and miracles will be made."

JEFF BOMBERGER

With our shamanic facilitator still drumming and vivid impressions still playing out in my mind, tears began to stream from my closed eyes and down my cheeks. In that moment, I felt an overwhelming sensation of love, warmth, and acceptance fill my entire being. It was like an anvil that had been lodged in my chest was suddenly lifted, and I had a transcendent experience of wholeness. The Japanese have a word, *yūgen*, which is an awareness of the universe that triggers emotional responses in us that are too profound, too deep, and all too mysterious for words. In a moment that will remain with me for the rest of my waking life and beyond, while the shamanic drumbeat pulsed on, I felt myself consumed by what I imagine the Japanese would call *yūgen*, an awareness of all that is that was so profoundly deep, moving, and ineffable that all I could do was weep tears of joy.

After I sat with this feeling for who knows how long, I reengaged with the council in my mind:

>I thanked them. I asked, "Can I come back?"
>
>"Yes."
>
>"How often?"
>
>"As you see fit."
>
>I was then lowered down. Journeyed back.

In the time after, I could feel my heart cracked wide

open. My emotional and intuitive senses became extra sharp and heightened, even more than they had been before I joined the workshop. I couldn't help but be overwhelmed by a tremendous sense of gratitude for not just the revelation and the journey I'd experienced but all of life itself. This journey left me permanently transformed. It forever altered the way I view, receive, and interact with the world. It forever altered my commitment to breathing life into the higher spiritual ideals I hold deep in my heart.

I was awestruck by this journey, but not totally surprised. I'd flirted with fleeting experiences like this before, which made me realize that this experience may not have been possible if I had not been doing the work I'd been consistently doing before the workshop. I may not have had this experience if I had not been in tune with myself enough to know I was still ailing from a trauma-scarred heart. This transformation may not have been possible if I didn't have the courage and curiosity to explore unchartered spiritual territory that is largely misunderstood in our culture. This healing may not have been possible if I hadn't had an unwavering faith in our intrinsic connection to the divine itself and what I've come to call the soul force.

Which brings us to the material you're holding in your hands right now. The message of healing that came through for me that day is a relevant message for all of us. It is one of many messages and insights I've received both before and since that journey, which gently, consistently, and persistently compel me to go deeper into the vastness of our universal connection and uncover the intrinsic spiritual power at the disposal of all humanity.

As my spiritual practice has stretched and expanded what is possible for me, I have been guided through my work with soul force to help stretch and expand the possibilities for others. It is my intention for our time together to be a source of inspiration for you on your journey with your own spirituality and personal growth. It is my intention that our exchange may, in some fashion, help you come to know what I call soul force for yourself in your own way and in your own time.

Take this book and my experiences within as nothing more than an offering, a gesture of goodwill without any expectation or requirement from me. I hope that you'll simply receive this material as an opportunity to explore, reflect, consider, and pursue whatever rings true for you. Take what serves you, and leave what does not. In keeping with the shamanic tradition as I've come to understand it, know that the only thing more important to me than my own direct revelation is your finding your path to direct revelation. It would certainly bring me great joy if your time with my words here aided your ability to touch soul force for yourself, but this is not an expectation I'll burden either of us with. I do sincerely want you to know your unique connection and expression of soul force as much as I yearn to know and express mine. For when we touch the truth of who we are for ourselves, the entire world transforms.

Who I am, who we all are at our core, is whole and divine. We have all experienced pain, we have all experienced trauma, and we have all suffered; yet we are not those experiences in and of themselves. We are so much more than a by-product of environmental and evolutionary circumstances. We are healers and creators. When we as individuals open ourselves up to the power of soul force, we will not only know who we are, but we will directly be shown we are so much more than we could possibly imagine. When we practice discipline and take steps toward connecting to our deepest, most authentic spiritual selves—when we wade forward into the darkness of the unknown with only the unshakeable faith in our inner light of soul force—miracles will be made.

There is only one thing left to do, and that's to take the first step toward awakening the soul force within. What do you say? Are you ready to discover soul force for yourself?

WHAT IS SOUL FORCE?

I know that the title of this book sounds like something that Yoda came up with. I don't mean to disappoint you, but everyone's favorite intergalactic sage didn't come up with the term *soul force*, and neither did I. I love to read and have a passion for words, but I am not in the habit of inventing new phrases like William Shakespeare. I'm simply not that cool. Like most who dabble in the humanities, I'm simply borrowing language that resonates with me and building on it in my own way. I only hope that I can in turn provide relatable stories, experiences, context, language, ideas, and spiritual practices that you feel compelled to borrow and build on in your own unique way.

Soul force is a phrase I am borrowing from Mohandas Gandhi and Dr. Martin Luther King Jr. In their efforts to liberate people from oppression and social suffering through nonviolence, they both used the phrase *soul force* to describe the transformative power of nonviolence. Their philosophy of clinging to what is true and transforming hate with love was ultimately inspired by the teachings of Jesus and his Sermon on the Mount.

And while we often look to cultural figures like Jesus, Gandhi, and King as models of inspired, moral, and spiritual living, I've come to understand that the subtle intuition, the power, and the moral authority that made these men historically larger than life are an integral part of who we are as human beings—each and every one of us. You and I, we don't need a mass nonviolent social movement or a worldwide religious following to recognize, awaken, and utilize the power of soul force within. We simply need the discipline and sincere desire to welcome it into our lives.

To be clear about what our time together is really going to be about, let's break down the phrase *soul force* into bite-size pieces. I want to illustrate my personal conception of soul force as I've come to interpret it and integrate it into my own life and then convey what soul force can mean for us if we fully embrace it as I've presented. First, let's define the words *soul* and *force* separately:

> **soul.** *The energetic essence, moral, and emotional nature of human beings.*
>
> **force.** *The capacity to do work and cause physical change, energy, strength, or active power.*

Soul force is the animating energy of all of life itself, and it is our ability to physically live and express the essence of our moral and emotional nature. Soul

AWAKENING SOUL FORCE

is the subtle energetic aspect of our being; it is the divine within. Force, then, is the active element of this energy—our divinity in motion. Soul force expresses itself as inspired thought, truthful word, and aligned action of the physical body. Soul force is made manifest when our lived truth aligns with the ultimate truth.

The soul is moral, emotional, and creative intelligence. It is pure consciousness itself. The soul is our highest self, which seeks the experience of love, peace, cooperation, harmony, and healing. This part of ourselves often speaks softly, but because it is unlimited and directly connected to our Creator, it is the most powerful aspect of who we really are. The soul is by and large the most consciously unfamiliar—yet most essential—part of ourselves. It is my hope that this material can in some way serve as a guide to strengthening our connection to this aspect of self and awaken us to the limitless power of soul force.

Soul force is intricately connected with another familiar aspect of self: the mind. The mind is the bridge between the etheric aspect of our soul and the dense material body. Information, ideas, inspiration, creativity, and thoughts originating from the soul can make their way into our conscious awareness by way of the mind. We often call this intuition, which is an expression of soul force. These movements of mind, which manifest as thoughts and feelings, can then inspire action expressed through the physical body. Have you ever thought about someone unexpectedly, so you call them to see how they are doing only to find out this person was just thinking about you too? That's intuition — that's soul force in motion. Can you think of a moment in your life where you suddenly were inspired to say or do something that turned out to be exactly what was needed in that moment?

I remember back when I first started driving, I was coming over the hill near my parents' house. At the top of the hill is a four-way stop that has pretty low visibility off to the left as you come up over the rise. One night, I was driving home late and pulled up to the stop sign. I looked left and right, and the coast seemed clear, but then something inside told me to wait. A second later, a car that was out of my line of sight sped into view and blew right through the stop sign at full speed. Had I not listened to that little hunch inside that had told me to wait a split second, I would have been sideswiped on the driver's side of my truck! I had not and could not have seen that car coming, yet the higher aspect of myself had. To hear that thought and to honor that thought had been to surrender to the intelligence of soul force. Have you ever had an experience like that?

On a less subtle level, our body experiences physical sensations as it touches, tastes, smells, hears, and sees a world outside itself. The environment and circumstances we experience impress information on the body, and this information, by way of the mind, becomes part of our conscious experience. Our environment and experiences shape a perception about who and what we are. Do you ever have self-doubt or self-defeating thoughts? We all do. Negative thought patterns can sometimes alter and drown out our connection to soul force. If we are out of tune with the truth of our soul and become encumbered by the thoughts, experiences, and impressions of the world coming from outside us, we can slip into a state of being disempowered and feeling like less than we truly are. If, on the other hand, we remain connected to our soul force and familiarize ourselves with it, we can move through the world empowered by the truth in all circumstances. The mind is a powerful tool, and it can serve one of two masters: the body or the soul. Ideally, we want it to serve both the body and soul at once. A mind overconsumed by spirit can render our body inert and static. A mind overconsumed by the sensations of the physical body can be stressed and spiritless. What we may aspire to achieve is the holistic integration of body, soul, and mind, to balance and harness their individual powers for the sake of self-mastery, increased awareness, and empowered living.

For our purposes of awakening soul force, we want to learn how to quiet and understand the mind so that we may get in touch with our soul vibration within.

JEFF BOMBERGER

We want to learn how to distinguish energy, thoughts, intuitions, and inspirations that originate within us from the energy, thoughts, and impressions we're soaking up from the world outside us. By becoming conscious of our essential nature and its relationship to the world, we can then begin the process of recalibrating and aligning our physical experience with the purest version of our soul's truth within us. When we learn how to allow the flow of information from our soul to be expressed through our thoughts, words, and the physical body, we open ourselves to more fully living our truth. When we learn how to accept and acknowledge the objective truth flowing from the outside world through us, we may enter into a more conscious and harmonious relationship with truth itself. At the end of the day, it is through the gift of this physical body that we breathe waking life into the essence of soul force by living our truth fully, wholly, and consistently out in the world. That is the ultimate destination if it is self-mastery we seek.

Soul force is always present whether we are aware of it or not. Its presence may be subtle and imperceptible if we have not yet learned to turn our undivided attention in its direction. Soul force also has the potential to be incredibly potent, creative, and transformative if we allow ample time and space for it to fully blossom in our awareness. Like building a thick set of Dwayne "the Rock" Johnson–sized spiritual biceps, the strength of our soul force and the degree to which it is expressed through our own individual mind, body, and spirit is going to be closely correlated with our personal intentions to nurture, understand, and grow this soul power for ourselves. Muscles grow with proper exercise, healthy nutrition, and ample rest and recovery. Think of our journey ahead as an experiment in finding the exercises and nutrients that will help you grow your personal soul force as strong as it can possibly be. Are you ready to be a powerful force of love and truth?

You may already have a number of techniques, exercises, and practices you utilize to connect to your soul and quiet your mind. If so, hooray! Hopefully the information I am going to share with you can be used to supplement or complement what you're already doing. Praying, saying the rosary, practicing yoga, and using passage meditation are some of the many ways you may already be reaching out and forging a connection with your soul and the divine. You may also be very adept at expressing soul force without being completely aware of it. Whether you're a doting parent, a volunteer for a cause you care about, a truth-seeking college student, or an inspired artist, you may already be expressing your highest truth in your own unique and subtle ways. However, this process of expansion and expression is eternal and endless. My goal is to remind and inspire you to trust your soul impulses and to empower you to live the truth of who you really are in this world as earnestly and consistently as you possibly can so that we can all enjoy the beauty of your spiritual awakening.

Are you still not sure where or what this soul force is and how to find it? Where you find the truth, you will find soul force. Where you find your highest vision and your grandest ideal, you will find soul force. Where you find the feelings of joy, expansion, and inspiration, you will find soul force. Where you find healing and transformation, you will find soul force. Where broken things become whole, you will find soul force. Where your voice shakes speaking your naked truth to power, you will find soul force. Where you find the strength to move hearts, minds, and mountains, you will find soul force. Where you find the most authentic expression of your mind, body, and spirit, you will find soul force. Most fundamentally, you will find soul force by simply looking at the power of love within yourself.

I want you to think back to a moment in your life when you felt in total alignment. A moment when your mind, soul, and body all came together to express your truth in the world. A moment when you were called to acknowledge an unshakeable inner knowing that you felt deep in the marrow of your bones. Maybe you had an impulse to stand up to a bully or take an unexpected risk. Maybe you had a deep gut instinct about a person, a place, a job, or an activity. Maybe you sprung into compassionate, caring action for a friend in need. Maybe you walked away from a toxic relationship. Whatever situation comes to mind, take a moment to fully remember that experience—the thoughts that ran through your mind, the feelings that flowed through your body. Recall the sensations urging you, "Go! Go! Go!" or "No! No! No!" What were you feeling called to do? What action did you take? What did it feel like to betray or honor that deep inner sense? When have you experienced thinking, speaking, or living your deepest truth? When can you say you have felt the subtle but powerful influence of soul force in your life?

AWAKENING SOUL FORCE

INSPIRATION

By the end of August 2018, I had started to feel a deep inner pull to get quiet. Life was insanely busy. In the tarot card readings I was doing for myself, I repeatedly pulled the hermit card—a card of solitude, spiritual seeking, and being open to higher wisdom. The hermit card in Kim Krans's the Wild Unknown tarot deck depicts a turtle hunkered down in its shell under a single darkness-illuminating lamp resting on its back. The card spoke to me. "What I wouldn't give to be that turtle for a while!" I would think every time I pulled it. Late in the evenings, when the frenetic hubbub of the daily grind would simmer down, I was more regularly being drawn to journey and sit with my yellow legal pads. I was no stranger to these impulses. I am a fishy little Piscean after all, an astrological sign known for intuition and psychic connection. Putting my pen to paper and letting pure thought flow was a practice I had become intimately familiar with when I was a teenager. This time around, the quality of sensations running through my being as I channeled my

JEFF BOMBERGER

meditations felt more intense than normal. Information began to come more regularly than in years past. The insights and revelations coming through were grounded, deep, and often profound in their simplicity.

October 16, 2018

The past is present, and the present is past. Healing must occur. Wounds must be mended with tender love, compassion and awareness. You must do the work to dissociate yourself with the mental and emotional formations with which you've become accustomed to and clear space for transformation and new beginnings.

Who you really are is not suffering, but pure, blissful and creative joy. The importance of healing your wounded child cannot be understated. Do not feel embarrassed or ashamed that you want to indulge in childlike pursuits. Do not judge yourself for the wholesale rejection of any "shoulds" in your life that do not align with your statement about who you wish to be in this world.

If your inner child is calling, answer the call. Go play. Pick up the phone, coordinate a pick-up game, and go play! Allow yourself to breathe. Allow yourself to thrive. You are the only one who can be a guardian of your wellness. No one will do it for you. No one

AWAKENING SOUL FORCE

is feeling your feelings for you. No one is sensing what you sense for you. Be expressive. Be honest. Be vulnerable.

Most importantly, be playful. Seek joy! List out what brings you joy. Spend more time doing those things. Spend more time in your bliss. Be the arbiter of your bliss, the defender of joy and the creator of light! That is who you really are. Just remember, to "be" that, you must "be" there. You must be.

The more messages like this came through, the more I wanted to give myself the space to retreat into my lamp-lit turtle shell. At this particular point in time, I was creating all of the digital and branded content for then-congressional-candidate Katie Hill as well as for PATH (People Assisting the Homeless), a nonprofit working to end homelessness in the state of California. On the political side, we had just shot a new round of commercials for Katie's campaign, and we were pressing to create content for a big, final push in one of the most hotly contested congressional races in the country. On top of that, PATH was running its big end-of-the-year fund-raising campaign, for which I was also creating a series of minidocumentaries featuring successfully housed clients. The spiritual call to get quiet was coming in loud and clear, and I did what I thought was my best—meditating daily, journeying when I could, and making time to quiet the mind.

The truth of the matter is, I was entangled in so much physical activity and traveling that I was not able to adequately process the roller coaster of emotions I found myself experiencing and powering through day in and day out. Late night seemed like the only time quiet enough for clarity and personal revelation to emerge unencumbered by the energy and emotions of other people. I could feel something brewing. I sensed myself winding down the end of a two-year period that had been by far more creative, more physically productive, and in a lot of ways more spiritually transformative than any I had experienced in my life thus far. I had gone through a mix of blissful highs matched by painful lows condensed so closely together that I rarely had time to ride any single emotion for too long . . . until the end of the year struck.

My nearly two-year stint on the campaign eventually came to a positive end. Katie Hill was elected to Congress as the first woman to ever represent our district, and I was enjoying a brief hiatus from creating content for PATH as well. Despite these two massive projects being wrapped, I still did not feel settled and refreshed. Days after Christmas and right before the New Year, I finally broke. I had a complete nervous breakdown that shook me to my core. My partner and I had an intense blowup that sent my physical and emotional body into a dizzying state of temporary disarray. In a tsunami of pent-up emotions, my physical body shook, trembled, and all but collapsed as I found I could no longer keep it all together. I fell into a deep, temporary depression and was completely disinterested in most human interaction. For the first time in years, I wasn't particularly motivated to pick up my camera or sit at my editing bay. Talking to people felt draining and laborious. I was feeling incredibly raw and even more hypersensitive to emotions and energy than normal. What I desired more than anything in that particularly dim moment was to be alone with myself and spirit. I wanted to do nothing. I wanted to be nothing at all. I was ready to retreat into my shell and submit to the call of the hermit.

What transpired over the next several months might seem almost paradoxical, but it was nothing short of extraordinary from my own perspective. Feeling emotionally depleted and energetically exhausted, I allowed myself to simply "be" as much as I possibly could. I of course tended to those earthly matters that kept food on the table, but I predominantly focused my energy and attention on setting aside the time to open up to whatever was waiting to burst out of me. What emerged was twofold. First, I finally had the time and space to fully reconcile and process emotional wounds that were still open deep in my heart. Over the course of the prior two years, I had not allowed myself to mend from a series of experiences that had made me feel dishonored and taken advantage of. There was unresolved pain from an experience of betrayal by a close friend. We'd made amends, but I'd never really allowed myself to acknowledge how painful that particular experience had been for me. I decided to dive into that and explore it.

There were also unresolved issues from an onslaught of several professional violations—from having ideas blatantly stolen to being verbally denigrated by someone who was supposed to be a colleague—still percolating deep in my emotions. I needed time to process these experiences. Not surprisingly, many of these feelings mirrored lower octaves of experiences I've been repeatedly faced with in my life. I am hypersensitive to big egos, bullies, and those who abuse their power. This is an archetype that has reared its head often in my life: as a vindictive youth baseball coach, as an emotionally abusive spouse, as a tyrannical television producer, and as a toxically behaving spiritual guru. When I see anyone as the target of another person's self-serving, manipulative power trip, it makes me incredibly angry. This is a massive personal trigger for me, and having to face this archetype in my life has taught me a lot about grace, about power, and about learning how to deal with injustices with integrity.

My heart was also aching from losing an incredibly dear and intimate relationship with my sister's family as she and her little kiddos had moved across the country rather unexpectedly and abruptly. To top it all off, I found old trauma from my divorce cropping up in my current relationship as well. Part of what came roaring out when I finally got quiet was the kind of icky stuff we forget to look at and sit with honestly because we're too busy doing rather than being.

On an unbelievably positive note, most of the material contained in this book gushed out of me like a geyser over the same time period. The first draft poured from the depths of my heart over the course of five weeks in the New Year. It was as if my call to be still served both a powerful individual and collective purpose. I had just needed to be still enough to process my own emotions and heal my own wounds, which were clearly in need of attention. In retrospect, I am beyond thankful for the time I afforded myself to move through that healing experience. Parallel to this deep shift I was undergoing, I was simultaneously opening up to a wealth of psychic and spiritual information that expanded upon the nearly two decades of spiritual self-knowledge that I'd been accumulating, both consciously and unconsciously, since I was a teenager. Which brings us to today—to this perfect time and this perfect space for us to have a meaningful, reflective, and philosophical exchange about the truth of our humanity, our spirit, and the nature of soul force as I've come to experience it. This book is my answer to an inner call to share my own personal dance with soul force, for the sake of cracking open a dialogue about living our highest truth together.

I am more convinced than ever that we need a spiritual revolution in our hearts. I'm proud of the public work I've done professionally, creatively, socially, and politically, but, in the depths of my soul, I know that the true transformation that awaits each one of us is a spiritual one. I have to admit my life path has been rather unconventional, but it's certainly never been boring! I've been fortunate to have a variety of unique life experiences in many different industries and social circles, and I was led to each experience by the intuitive pull of my soul force. I've participated in high school and college sports, worked as an actor in Hollywood as a child and an adult, served as a fitness professional for over a decade, been arrested on the US Capitol steps, worked on several political campaigns, run for Congress myself, taken shamanic journeys, and now somehow found myself writing, shooting, directing, and editing digital content for a living. My journey has been at times conscious and deliberate and other times not so conscious, naive, and even clumsy. There have been plenty of plot twists and turns, hard lessons, and marvelous revelations alike, some of which I'll share with you throughout this book.

Now that I have shared what inspired me and brought me to this moment here with you, I'd love for you to take

AWAKENING SOUL FORCE

a moment to consider what brought you to this book in this time and in this space. How did you come to be here sitting with these words? What harmony are you searching for? What do you hope to get from reading this material? Think about the timing of this book—about how and when it has arrived in your life. What's going on right now that makes this the perfect moment to slow down, reconnect with your inner truth, and awaken the soul force within you?

THE PATH AHEAD

Everything in this book stems from my own personal experience, which means it is a reflection of what is true for me. I am my own spiritual and moral authority, and so are you. What I mean by that is, at the end of the day, it's up to us to take full responsibility for our lives. It is our spiritual right and our obligation to ourselves and to the universe to live life in accordance with that which is true for us, in our own lived experiences. The common destination we all share on this path is awakening to the truth of who we really are, truth in the world, and the power of soul force at our disposal; how we get there will be unique for each of us. Therefore, the path we're going to walk together throughout this experience is to be regarded as a collaboration rather than a competition.

I am going to share personal stories about my own journey and provide information about spiritual thought, energy work, healing, psychic phenomena, and a litany of meditative and reflective practices that I've come to cherish in my own personal discipline. My stories are simply meant to be relatable illustrations and examples of what my spiritual experience has been and has meant to me. Hopefully, you will connect with these stories in a way that enhances your own spiritual journey in one way or another. If not, that's OK! The exercises, practices, and suggestions I make in this book are not the be-all and end-all of the subject matter and should be treated as merely windows into my own experience in each respective arena. I am not writing this book to tell you what to do or how to experience your life or your spirituality but rather to offer up potential pathways to awakening soul force for yourself. I'm simply a version of life, expressed in my own unique way, and I want you to find your version of life, expressed in your own unique way.

You may resonate with some—or all—of what I share in this book, or you may not. Take what works, and build on it in your own way. Feel free to toss out the rest. Your path is yours to seek, discover, and explore as you find what is true for you and step fully into awakening soul force within.

SOUL-FORCE BEGINNINGS

When I was twelve years old, I saw my first psychic reader. It was a drizzly southern California day, and my dad and I had stopped by a tiny new age shop called the Psychic Eye to pass some time and seek refuge from the rain. As we stepped inside, I was greeted by the smell of incense, sage, and other hippie-dippie scents that I couldn't quite place. The shelves were lined with a variety of crystals, tarot card decks, Buddhas, and earthy trinkets, and the doorways had strings of beads dangling from the threshold to the floor, separating the public space from the private reading rooms. My dad and I decided to each have a private tarot reading done with a woman named Pamela, who I was 100 percent convinced was going to break out a crystal ball. Much to my dismay, she didn't have a crystal ball, but she did have something special to offer us on that damp southern California day.

Even though she had never met us before, Pamela honed in on impeccable details about our lives, our hearts, and our minds. My extremely skeptical father and my curious twelve-year-old self both walked out believing something really unique had just transpired.

JEFF BOMBERGER

One thing I remember Pamela distinctly telling me was that when I looked at myself in the mirror, I saw a player on the Rams (one of my favorite football teams), but she saw me working with people as a healer. I remember thinking that this was absolute crazy talk because in my mind I was going to play in the NFL and grow up to be a big role model for starry-eyed kids like me someday. This woman who had never met me before somehow knew that this was my heart's desire, and yet she ultimately saw me as something I didn't even understand at the time. A healer? It wasn't until I was well on my own journey of spiritual self-discovery that I would come to recognize what her prophecy had meant decades earlier.

When I left that day, I couldn't stop wondering: What had this lady seen? Where had these visions come from? How had this woman I'd never met before known my dreams? Was what she had said going to be true? If so, how? This experience sparked my own initial curiosity in psychic phenomena as well as metaphysics, and I've been seeking ever since. As I mentioned earlier, my first, self-initiated spiritual practice was lying down and doing guided meditations to John Edward's *Unleashing Your Psychic Potential* cassette tape. On nights when I was feeling anxious and stressed, I would pop that tape in my sticker-riddled boom box and drift into alternate states of consciousness. The guided meditations helped me ease my anxious thoughts around my week of foot-

AWAKENING SOUL FORCE

ball successes and failures. I discovered I had a knack for the whole visualizing thing and that I was able to easily create very vivid, detailed images in my imagination that would bring calming effects to my mind and body. This was the first time I was taught how to connect to divine white light and let it consume me. Seeking this connection always refreshed me, and I often returned to it when I was feeling heavy, negative, and totally out of sorts. An iteration of this meditation is a practice I now use daily, which I refer to as going to the well for rejuvenation (we'll talk more about this later). These formative experiences laid the foundation for much of the material we're going to discuss on our journey to understanding our connection to soul force.

In high school, my younger sister, Kristi, showed demonstrable signs of a highly accurate psychic sense, and I straggled behind as a little less gifted in this particular area. In fact, I was so enamored with sports at that age that I often lagged behind my gifted sister in both intellectual and spiritual pursuits. As a family, we experimented with tarot cards. We would do readings for one another while referencing the little Rider-Waite booklet of card descriptions that had come with it. I mostly thought that the cards and their symbols were interesting and mysterious; I certainly wasn't making plans to quit my dream of professional sports. Every so often, my dad would play these inventive "psychic games" with Kristi and me. He'd put something—like a piece of jewelry, a family picture, or a question he'd written down—in an envelope or a box, and then he'd tell us to go meditate on whatever it was and write down what came to us. My sister consistently showed a remarkable aptitude for tapping into information that was emotionally relevant to whatever was hidden from us. To my surprise, I noticed that over time and with practice, I began to regularly get very clear images and sensations on matters related to the physical aspects of what was hidden, such as shapes, colors, and other physical qualities and characteristics.

For example, one night my dad asked us to meditate on what was in the big box he held in his hands. We weren't allowed to touch or handle the box; he just held it up for us to see. My sister and I then retreated to our rooms, did our little meditation, and wrote down what came to us. As usual, Kristi honed right in on the love and intimacy tied to the ring that was in the box, through an elaborate daydream of roses and ceremonies that filled her mind's eye. What I saw was different. I got the color gold in my meditation, saw the inside of a metal loop, and got a very clear sense of a closed circle. We were both surprised when my dad revealed to us that we were meditating on his gold wedding band. Truthfully, it was always tough for me to discern what a psychic "hit" felt like and what was just my imagination, so I usually accepted my successes rather skeptically. It did seem my sister and I were tapping into something, though. Where did this information come from? What were we tapping into? While I couldn't answer those questions, this was really the beginning of my being convinced that we as human beings are connected to an expanded awareness that is far beyond our limited physical experience. As I've come to now understand, we were experiencing what it is like to connect to soul force.

Around this same time, our country endured the 9/11 terrorist attacks. Obviously, what ensued after this national tragedy is still ongoing history for America, but, personally, what followed for me had a profound impact on my spiritual development. In the time before our military invaded Iraq, I was what I'd call "teenager aware" of what was going on in Afghanistan. I'd catch a bit about the war in class, or I'd sometimes inadvertently pick up information from newsclips while popping in and out of the house. In my mind, our military was over there trying to catch some people who had done some really horrible things over here. That was about as deep and complex as it got for my football-focused brain back then. My parents were not political, so there was never chatter about politics or the war around the house. In fact, most of our discussions revolved around day-to-day happenings—Mom and Dad's work life, school, football, hopes, and dreams. My family ate dinner together every night, and we'd often get into discussions about spirituality and philosophy. We'd also regularly veer into analyzing dreams for one another. Truthfully, I wasn't paying attention to the United States' involvement in the Middle East until I had a dream experience of my own that could now slide in as a topic of our dinner conversations.

One morning, I woke up from a normal night of sleep with an extraordinary sense that I had just witnessed something of mammoth importance. Visually, the dream wasn't quite a Steven Spielberg classic and lacked spectacular theatrics. In fact, for the entirety of the dream, I remained in a fixed point of view, as if I were an objective and omnipresent eye that never moved. From my vantage point, I could see that I was in a big room with distinct crown molding, and I was keenly aware of a palpable, high-stakes energy in the room. I was looking up as though through a glass table at a diverse group of men in suits. Although they were all different shapes, sizes, colors, and creeds, they had one thing in common: they felt powerful. There was a roar of chatter—some of it in languages I did not understand. Men shuffled around the table, and there was passionate, spirited discussion back and forth. Suddenly, a big map was sprawled out over my point of view, and I could faintly see the outlines of countries drawn on what I recognized to be a map of the world. Some fingers pointed to a spot near the center of the map, which felt like

AWAKENING SOUL FORCE

Egypt to me, and suddenly a voice, in an indiscernible accent, very audibly pronounced, "He's going to do it without us. It doesn't matter what we say; he's going to go in by himself. He's going to do it." Then I woke up.

The dream was perplexing to me at first. The language was vague, but it definitely felt like a slice of very important life. The experience as a whole carried with it a residual sense of weight and incredible significance that haunted me for weeks. Unable to shake the feeling that this was important, I followed an impulse to begin watching the news on a daily basis. A few weeks after I had this dream, President Bush announced unilateral action in Iraq, against the consent of the United Nations and NATO. My gut sank when I saw this newscast. When I had had the dream, I had not been apprised of what was going on overseas, but I'd paid enough attention in school to know what the UN and NATO were. This revelation packed a wallop I'll never forget. In that moment, I immediately knew what my "random" dream full of men in suits was about. To this day, I consider this my first major wake-up call to a heightened collective awareness. This message not only called me to expand my awareness of dreams and spirituality, but it also provided me a glimpse into humanity's global connection at a deeper, more subtle level.

What ensued afterward was about a month of dreaming about the war overseas. Sometimes these were very long, drawn-out dreams. Some of them depicted combat missions that I would experience from a first-person point of view. Others were more like living still-life photos or omniscient impressions and experiences. The real kicker was that within a few days of these sleep-time experiences, I would see the exact same imagery in news footage on the television. The composition and framing of a particular shot would often be identical, as well as the action caught on tape, significant landmarks, and minor details. Being a junior in high school, I really didn't know what to say or do with the information. What could I do? I definitely didn't talk about it with my teachers or any of my friends. To them, I was just a passionate athlete who wanted to lift weights, crush spring workouts, and play Division I football someday. The visuals that were coming through were eerily accurate, and overall the sensation these dreams left me with was too profound to deny. I did, however, tell the only people I felt like I could tell: my family. When it came to this specific series of dreams, I settled on doing the only thing I felt like a teenager could do, and I simply started paying attention.

My teenage years were the beginning of my now long and intimate journey exploring the nature of the soul. As I will share in the coming chapters, the pursuit of inner and outer truth and spiritual knowledge became an unyielding drive for me, and the fire continues to

AWAKENING SOUL FORCE

burn deep within me to this day. By the time I hit the age of eighteen, there was no turning back. I dove headfirst into any piece of literature I could get my hands on related to spirituality, philosophy, and higher wisdom. I began to formally study philosophy and the world's religions in college. I had—and still have—a particular affinity for Eastern traditions and the teachings of Jesus. Outside of class, I consumed ideals and wisdom shared by the likes of Paramahansa Yogananda, Thich Nhat Hann, and Jiddu Krishnamurti. Years of practice and self-discipline culminated with my shamanic journey, which revealed to me the wholeness of myself and all others. Throughout the entirety of this material, you're likely going to hear a lot of concepts and ideas you may have heard before. As I've come to learn, repetition is key in our evolution, and universal truth manages to always find its way into our hearts if we intend to find it. It is my deepest hope that my affection for matters of the soul will somehow ignite a similar passion in you. Without further ado, I welcome you into my world and invite you to join me on a journey with soul force.

CLINGING TO TRUTH

―⚬⚬⚬―

The religion of nonviolence is not meant merely for the rishis and saints. It is meant for the common people as well. Nonviolence is the law of our species as violence is the law of the brute. The spirit lies dormant in the brute and he knows no law but that of physical might. The dignity of man requires obedience to a higher law—to the strength of the spirit.

—Gandhi

A core component of Gandhi's philosophy of nonviolence was satyagraha, or clinging to truth. Clinging to truth requires us to seek and honor truth without condition, both inside and outside us. After all, it has been said that the truth shall set us free, has it not? This requires us to refrain from lying—especially to ourselves. This requires us to acknowledge reality as it is. Honesty with ourselves and others is crucial to living an empowered life. This kind of integrity gives us the strength to live in accordance with dimensions of higher love and wisdom deep inside of us. In our efforts together, we are going to use our intuition, the power of observation, and self-analysis to find our way into the depths of spiritual truth. By seeking truth, clinging to it, and refraining from being dishonest with ourselves and the world, we can become empowered beyond measure. By clinging to truth, we may dissolve illusions that trap us in negative beliefs, self-destructive patterns, and violent behavior, clearing for us a path to enter into a life that is more firmly aligned with soul force.

Soul force is our unique connection to and expression of the universal vibration of love—the spiritual nature from which we came and to which we shall return. As individuals, we are a unique manifestation of this vibration, and we are granted the opportunity to breathe life into its flesh and blood existence every single day. A way into embodying this love force is through becoming familiar with the soul and growing our intuitive faculties.

Mahatma Gandhi and Dr. Martin Luther King Jr. both famously relied on soul force to liberate the people of their time from the crushing weight of social oppression. For our purposes, we will focus on liberating ourselves from our own experience of oppression, suffering, personal trauma, and the energy blocks we experience within. Instead of intending to change the world outside of us, we are first going to open ourselves to being transformed by quiet soul force from the inside out. In this way, soul force is healing in nature.

AWAKENING SOUL FORCE

On my path, I've created a few core intentions for myself to help keep me aligned with soul force. The following principles guide me like a moral constellation etched in my heart. In my ongoing inquiry into myself and in my effort to welcome the healing and transformative qualities of soul force into my life, it is my intention always:

- to know myself honestly and see myself clearly so that I may also see the world clearly;

- to open my heart and mind enough to allow direct experience of soul force to touch me personally; and

- to see myself, others, and the totality of this world through the soul-force-inspired eyes of love and healing.

Take a moment to consider the intentions I've laid out for myself and see how they resonate with you. What kind of intentions would you like to set for yourself on this journey with higher wisdom? As you walk this path, what sort of commitments would you like to make to yourself in an effort to discover, experience, and strengthen soul force on your own? If you could create a few guiding principles for yourself on your spiritual quest, what would they be? To honor what's in your heart? To trust your gut? To follow the path of love?

JEFF BOMBERGER

Sit for a few minutes and jot down any and all intentions or guiding principles that want to be expressed through you right now. Use your own words. Find your own language. That is part of the important work we're up to!

With sincere intention, we can begin the process of bringing spirit and healing into being by expressing it in our daily lives. If we fixate on shining a light on the brightest and darkest parts of ourselves, we may begin to realize our true spiritual nature. Our role and responsibility in the great collective blossoming of divine nature truly begins and ends with us. As long as we remain committed to tending our own spiritual garden, so to speak, and remain diligently dedicated to truth and love, the energetic ripple effect of this work will find its own way, in its own time, throughout the world at large. This is our opportunity to embrace what it means to be the change we wish to see in the world. When we liberate ourselves, we liberate the world. Finally, I'll have us remember that this self-directed spiritual call to action is nothing new: "Ask, and it shall be given you; seek, and ye shall find; knock, and it shall be opened unto you: For every one that asketh receiveth; and he that seeketh findeth; and to him that knocketh it shall be opened" (Matt. 7:7–8).

SOUL-FORCE FOUNDATIONS

He is like a man which built an house, and digged deep, and laid the foundation on a rock: and when the flood arose, the stream beat vehemently upon that house, and could not shake it: for it was founded upon a rock.

—Luke 6:48

You are pure energy.

You are your own soul authority.

You, your life, your spirituality, and your connection to soul force are your own responsibility to discover, explore, honor, cherish, and grow.

These are rocks of truth you may build your spiritual house on. No one is going to walk this path for you. No one can intuitively find your way into your own unique connection with soul force for you. No one else can be the divine experiencing itself as you. That's your job. This is not to say we won't have earthly and spiritual mentors to help us along the way. At the end of the day, though, it is ultimately up to us to forge our own spiritual path to realizing the loving awareness deep within us. It is our responsibility to learn the lessons we are meant to learn in the way we're meant to learn them. This in turn allows us to organically grow as we were meant to grow and to achieve the spiritual insight and wisdom we are destined to grasp for ourselves. Our essential life force does not manifest itself as a one-size-fits-all dogma; this would be incredibly boring and limiting for the unlimited! Therefore, we must be vigilant in pursuit of our soul-force connection and open up to the unlimited power waiting to be realized and materialized through us. On our journey together, I am going to consistently encourage us to honor some basic soul-force principles that I have found useful for creating the space for soul force to enter into my life.

Question everything that separates us from soul force

Soul force is the vibration of love. It is intuitive, creative, and free. Society will cloud our vision of ourselves and our connection to soul force. We are going to question the culture of our upbringing that separates us from these qualities. We are going to question the divisive culture in our household, at school, in the workplace, in sports, or within social clubs. We are going to question the news and our politicians that try to drive a wedge between ourselves and loving awareness. An incredible amount of physical, psychological, emotional, and spiritual damage is done when we don't do our due diligence and seek the truth. We must question the beliefs imposed upon us by authority figures, dogmas, and mass culture as these perspectives don't always align with soul force. We don't have to be crass about our questioning; we just have to be vigilant for the sake of truth and clarity. We must indiscriminately question everything that would have us separate ourselves from our inner wisdom, our intuition, our creativity, and our freedom.

Always seek what is true

We must relentlessly pursue truth. We'll aim to get to the bottom of things as much as we can — most fundamentally, ourselves. When truth becomes our destination, illusions and misconceptions fall by the wayside. The truth is an immovable and impenetrable force. It simply is. There is no justification necessary, no explanation needed. It just is. We will seek what is true versus what is not true. We will aim to find the truth for ourselves and try to look at the entire picture. Remember, the left wing and the right wing belong to the same bird. To see the whole picture — the bird for the bird — that is seeing with soul force.

Truth is the foundation upon which we must build up our soul force so that it grows undeniably strong. The truth can be ignored, it can be mocked, and it can be fought, but it does not vanish. It persists. We must fixate our eyes, our hearts, our minds, and our spirits on what is true whether what we see is magnificently beautiful or horrendously ugly. It is all one. To see this without judgment is to see with soul force. By seeking truth, we can attain knowledge and understanding and then, in turn, facilitate healing and reconciliation. With this knowledge and understanding, we gain a mastery of ourselves that truly sets us free.

Honor what is true

What good is discovering the truth if it is not honored? Accepting what is true empowers us by putting us in the position to decide how we wish to be in relation to whatever fact of life. Honoring what is true gives us great power. If we are deeply sensitive beings, and someone we love speaks harmful words to us but we say nothing, then we suffer. Yet if we acknowledge our truth and give voice to it, we can then begin a process of reconciliation with the other person by opening up a discussion about how we can more cooperatively interact. We may even learn something about this other person's truth in the process. If we honor the truth for both people, then we may choose to work with one another to alleviate this pain. We can even choose whether or not we want to remain in close relationship with that person at all given these truths. Acknowledging and honoring what is true gives us freedom. It also grants freedom to those we're in relationships with. Seeking what is true and honoring said truth is a path to liberation.

Do our best in each moment

We all hit potholes and step into proverbial buckets from time to time, and that's totally OK. We're constantly learning, growing, and evolving. If we always do the best with what we've got, given where we're at in the here and now, then we create space to be compassionate and forgiving toward ourselves and others by accepting things as they are in this moment. If we gave a calculus problem to a student who had only the knowledge of basic addition and subtraction, could we judge this student for not being able to solve the calculus equation? If we gave a student only half of the alphabet and told them to read us a story, could we judge them for their inability to read the story to us? No. The students in our examples don't have all the tools in their toolbox to solve these problems yet. But with patience, compassion, time, and effort and through a good amount of trial and error, they'll eventually attain adequate knowledge and apply it appropriately.

We are students on our journey to soul force. Along the way, we'll gather tools and knowledge that makes us more capable in all aspects of life. We must simply give our best and be open to learning as much as we can from each and every experience—the good, the bad, the ugly, the happy, and the sad. If we're open to the lessons of our experiences, the understanding we seek will find its way into our awareness and bring us into alignment with soul force.

Be more aware today than yesterday

Opening ourselves up to being more aware today than we were yesterday propels us forward on an upward spiral of expanded soul-force awareness. Being more aware today than yesterday keeps us engaged in an endless reflective process of discovery. By constantly expanding our awareness of ourselves in relationship to the world, we increase the possibilities and potentials for exponential and experiential growth. Experience gifts us with knowledge, and where we harvest knowledge and align it appropriately with the truth we seek and honor, we then give rise to wisdom. The goal is to end every day a little more open, a little more aware of ourselves, and a little wiser than we were when we woke up. If our focus remains fixed in this direction, the power and potency of soul force within knows no limits.

Live to heal

Let's move through this soul-force process with the intention of living to heal—that is, living to reconcile contradictory, fragmented, and wounded parts of ourselves and others. This does not mean our actions won't, in certain cases, feel or appear harmful to others. Walking away from a friendship, quitting a job, taking a break from a lover—all of these soul-driven actions might make ourselves or others feel hurt. In some cases, we may even find ourselves on the other end of these experiences as others also embark on *their* soul-force journey. The path to healing, though honorable and virtuous, will be challenging when we actually walk through the process of mending wounds and reconciling imbalanced energy; yet these growing pains will pass, as they always do. Healing does not mean no feeling or no pain. Our liberation lies not in transcending our humanness but in integrating it with soul force so that we walk through the world with our body, mind, and soul aligned.

Our faith and our truth are going to meet situations where we must make challenging conscious choices about who we are in life's smallest and grandest moments. Sometimes these are easy choices; other times, they are not. This is by design and is meant to move us closer to soul force. Every moment is an act of self-definition. Expansion is on the other side of these moments, and we will grow more at peace with the process of our evolution as our spiritual lens becomes larger.

If we live to heal, we will never act out of malice or with the intent to harm ourselves or another. With this perspective, we'll recognize that it is OK to have differences. It is OK to be on different paths. And what we'll realize on this healing path is that if we seek and honor the truth openly, lovingly, and compassionately, the healing vibration of soul force will take care of itself for us.

Finally, I want to give you a chance to think about any guiding principles that you currently lean on to set your moral compass. What spiritual mantras, sayings, texts, or passages resonate with you? Do you have a set of mantras, prayers, or teachings you feel are particularly helpful for guiding you on your current journey with truth and spirituality? The Golden Rule? Occam's razor? The Five Pillars? *The Four Agreements*? *The Secret*? The Beatitudes? The Four Noble Truths? The Eightfold Path? The prayer of Saint Francis? Or perhaps you have taken the time to craft your own guiding principles. Now would be a great moment to consider those ideals that you hold. Write them down and give them some attention. How present are these values in your daily thoughts, words, and deeds? Once you've spent some time reflecting on your moral guideposts, let's take our first big step into connecting with soul force.

CONSCIOUS BREATHING

Smile, breathe, and go slowly.

—Thich Nhat Hanh

A morning breeze causes the leaves outside to gently flutter about. The trees sound like an orchestra of soothing baby rattles dancing outside your window. You roll over onto your shoulder. The sun peeks through the blinds and kisses your sleepy face. You reach onto the bedside table and tap your phone. The display lights up: 9:32 a.m.

It's been one hell of a week. You got that massive project you were supposed to finish done right on time, and now it's time to relax. You could not be more relieved to finally have the chance to sleep in on this Saturday morning. You click the home button to open your phone just to make sure no one's trying to get ahold of you. No calls. No texts. Not even an unread email bubble in sight.

Thank. God.

You put the phone down and lazily roll over onto your back. You take a moment as you stare at the hypnotic swirling of the fan above. A bird gently chimes outside your window. The peace and quiet couldn't be more welcome today. You close your eyes and begin to think about all the time you have to do exactly nothing. Feels great, doesn't it?

Suddenly, you're startled by the horrendous vibrating on your nightstand. Despite the disruption, you remember today is the start of your well-deserved weekend, so you calmly reach over and pick up your phone. It's probably your friend . . . wait. Your boss?

You freeze a moment as your brain searches at a hundred miles an hour for the reason they might be calling. Then it hits you. You forgot one last finishing touch on the project. Immediately, your heart rate shoots through the roof. Your palms start to sweat. In a rush of panic, you begin to imagine your boss on the other end of the line, primed to rage at you for being terrible at your job. The phone continues to ring, only now it seems to be growing louder. Your mind races: "Man, I messed up. I'm such a loser. I can't believe I did that. This is the end of my project, my career . . . oh my god, my life is over!"

What should you do next?

If I were you, I'd breathe.

In Hinduism, breath is called prana. Prana is considered to be the nourishing, sustaining life force of the mind and body. As long as you are breathing, you are alive, and that alone is a gift to be eternally grateful for.

AWAKENING SOUL FORCE

The breath is healing, revitalizing, and rejuvenating. It purifies the mind and the body with every inhale and exhale. Not only can it be the calming force that we cling to in a spontaneous moment of crisis, but it can also be the steady anchor that centers our awareness in the here and now, in every moment of every day.

Take a moment to think about how often you currently engage in conscious breathing, if at all. Then try this simple conscious breathing exercise:

Take a moment to turn your attention to your breath right now, in this moment. Are you breathing in through your nose or your mouth? Are you exhaling out your nose or your mouth? Are your breaths shallow, like they're stuck in the upper part of your chest? Or are they deep and expansive in your diaphragm? What does your breath currently feel like? Is there anything about your breathing right now that is soothing, relaxing, or rejuvenating? Is there anything in your breathing that is energizing or enlivening?

Now purposefully take your next breath in through your nose. Turn your awareness to the sensation of the air as it passes through the nostrils when you inhale. Feel the air travel down into your body, expanding your belly slightly as your diaphragm fills up with breath. Your rib cage expands, and you feel your whole upper torso fill with air. When the breath feels full, exhale with the intention to empty all the air you just took in, slowly releasing the breath out your nose. Let your belly and your chest subtly fall.

Be conscious of the sensation of your chest collapsing as the breath leaves your body. After you have exhausted the breath, repeat this three or four times or as many times as you need to feel like you are conscious and aware and have a handle on your breathing. Don't worry about answering the phone yet; the boss can wait until after you've calmed your nervous system and balanced your breath. This simple technique of conscious breathing, turning your attention to your breath, can be done at any time in any moment of any day and can serve as an important regular practice all by itself. Don't just rely on it for when you feel stress coming on or you're emotionally aroused. Turn to conscious breathing when you're struck by the beauty of a mountainside, the laughter of a child, or the frolicking of a puppy. It's important to bring attention to our breath always because where our attention goes, energy flows.

Speaking of energy flowing, I want to introduce you to your soul force. Using the suggested conscious-breathing technique above, I want you to once again turn your attention to your breath. Focus on the sensation of the air as it flows into your nose and down into your body and fills your lungs with air. When you exhale, I want you to focus on the sensation of the breath leaving your body. Notice how the body gently relaxes as you expel

AWAKENING SOUL FORCE

all the breath within. Repeat this cycle three more times, focusing on the breath, clearing your mind, and settling into a more relaxed state of being.

Once you've completed your fourth round of breathing, I want you to take your hands and place them out in front of you about three to six inches apart. Turn your attention to the space between your palms. With your attention on this space between your hands, slowly begin to move your hands apart, as if a balloon were expanding between them. Move them only a couple inches, and then I want you to slowly bring them back together, as if the balloon between your hands is deflating. Repeat these motions again.

Do you feel that magnetic pull between your hands? Perhaps you even feel a tingling sensation. Welcome to soul-force energy! Take a moment to play with this energy. As you move your hands apart, feel it expand and grow between your hands. Bring your hands back together, and feel it contract and close in on itself. Have fun playing with this sensation. See how big you can grow it, how far you can feel its edges. Maybe even assign it a color (we'll delve deeper into the meanings of different colors later, so notice what color instinctively comes to mind). Sit with this vibration. Know it. Feel it. Trust it. And know that by engaging in conscious breathing, you also grow the strength and power of this vibration because it is the flow of soul force running through you.

JEFF BOMBERGER

The breath helps us tap into soul force.

As we embark on this journey, take some time to practice returning to your breath throughout the day. I suggest keeping a small journal with you (or taking notes on your phone, for my paperless pals) so that you can recount your experiences and track any patterns. Take note of what inspired you to check in with your breath. What emotions and thoughts were present? How did your body feel? What was the quality of your breath when you first noticed it? What was the quality of your breath once you spent some time conscious breathing? And finally, how did your body, thoughts, or emotions shift after spending this time with the breath?

Once you get the hang of turning your attention to your breathing, you're ready to continue on, as we build on the breath in our quest to know soul force for ourselves.

RHYTHMIC BREATHING

Inhale, and God approaches you. Hold the inhalation, and God remains with you. Exhale, and you approach God. Hold the exhalation, and surrender to God.

—Krishnamacharya

All of life is rhythm and vibration. That's why playing music makes for such wonderful metaphysical analogies when discussing matters of the universe. Rhythm, timing, and vibration are all key elements to manifesting harmony in music, and they are all key elements to manifesting harmony in life. On this journey, we venture to harmonize ourselves with the vibration of soul force. One fundamental element of this alignment begins with our breath, as we just discussed. Learning how to tune into our breath, control our breath, and welcome it into us in a conscious and loving manner can help us feel the presence of soul force within a matter of moments. Now I want us to take the next step and learn how to manipulate our breath specifically to connect to soul force. This technique is often referred to as rhythmic, or "pranic," breathing.

For this exercise, you may lie down, sit, or stand. A lot of meditation practices will encourage you to sit because posture is an important element of particular yogic practices. For me, I always have and still feel most comfortable meditating while lying down. Find what works best for you. I've never held the intention to become any particular kind of yogic or meditation master, and if you do, that's great; go ahead and pursue that. My intention has always been to find my most authentic and comfortable way into connecting with soul force, and I encourage you to do the same.

With rhythmic breathing, we're going to build on the awareness we've developed using conscious breathing by manipulating the breath in a controlled manner. We'll do this by counting the breath—inhaling to a count of six, holding at the top for a count of three, exhaling for a count of six, holding at the bottom for a count of three, and repeating this cycle several times. This will allow us to focus our minds on the breath itself and settle into a deep, meditative state.

Before I explain the full technique, it's important to know that when you first start this practice, your mind may drift off and begin daydreaming or thinking about other things. This is completely normal and nothing to stress about. If you notice your mind straying from the breath, simply refocus your attention on your breath and begin a new inhalation cycle.

AWAKENING SOUL FORCE

Another thing that sometimes happens is that you may begin to worry if you're doing the breathing "right." Again, this is totally normal, but please know that there is nothing to get right. Everything we're going to cover in this material is a practice, which means that you're going to do it over and over again. This also means that you'll get the chance to refine your skills more and more over time. Sitting down to engage with these exercises is about the intention to connect to soul force and getting into a habit of repeating the work. Like any new skill, what seems hard on the first day will become second nature weeks, months, and years down the road. Don't put too much pressure on yourself, and remember, this stuff is meant to liberate you from suffering, not be the source of it!

Finally, it is true that in the early trials with this technique, you may drift off into sleep once your body and mind begin to relax. Over time and with training, I've found it gets easier to harness control over your awareness. If you are going to sit, assume good posture by keeping your core tight, your chest up, and your head, neck, and shoulders as straight as possible. If you are sitting down, simply place your hands flat on your thighs, palms down, and relax your arms. If you're lying down or standing up, let your hands rest comfortably at your sides.

You are going to begin by taking a deep breath in

through your nose to the count of six, breathing into your stomach, expanding your lungs, and then filling that breath through the top of your chest. One. Two. Three. Four. Five. Six.

At the top of the sixth count, you are going to retain your breath in your slightly expanded belly and chest by holding for three counts. One. Two. Three.

Now you are going to exhale out your nose and slowly expel all the air out of your lungs to the count of six. One. Two. Three. Four. Five. Six.

At the end of the sixth count, you are going to refrain from breathing in for another count of three. One. Two. Three.

You are then going to repeat the deep inhale through your nose to the count of six and continue the full rhythmic cycle.

Pranic breathing is really a meditative practice all on its own, as your awareness remains solely focused and concentrated on your breath. This is an excellent way to ground yourself, clear your mind, and get centered at any moment of the day. I would suggest giving this exercise a try for three to five minutes to start; that way, you begin with a manageable amount of time that can be squeezed into the busiest of schedules. The great part about this kind of rhythmic breathing is that it can actually be practiced while moving through everyday life. You can turn your attention to conscious breathing while driving in the car, sitting on the bus, or walking the halls at work. There really is nothing stopping you from returning to your breath at any moment during the day.

I also wanted to introduce this rhythmic breathing early on because it will serve as the gateway into many of the meditative and self-reflective exercises included throughout the material. In fact, just about everything we're going to talk about in this book is profoundly more effective when we know how to focus our mind and turn inward at will. At the end of your rhythmic-breathing session, this is another great time to take your hands, rub them together, and hold them about three to six inches apart. Slowly move your hands away from one another, then slowly bring them back. Try this a few times, until you feel that magnetic sensation between your palms. This is an excellent way to bring your focus and attention to the pure soul force flowing through you.

SOUL-FORCE FIELD

It's your night out with your friends, and you're ready to blow off some steam. You're ecstatic about the comedy show you and your crew are about to catch at nine o'clock. One of your pals asks if they can catch a ride with you to meet the group down at the comedy club, and you happily oblige. After putting on your Saturday best and hitting the road, you swing by to grab your partner in crime. You pull up out front and give a friendly beep-beep on the horn to announce your arrival. Moments later, your friend frantically emerges from their place, phone tucked against their ear and visibly out of sorts.

As they climb into your car, you deliver up a cheerful "What's up!"

"Oh my god," your friend replies, and without even taking a breath, they launch into a toxic diatribe about a terrible date they had. Not wanting to miss the show, you put the pedal to the metal and head toward the venue.

A half hour drive goes by, and you arrive at the comedy club without having said anything since you muttered those fateful words, "What's up!" As you hand the parking attendant ten bucks, your friend finally begins to wrap up their epic rant.

"Thank you so much for listening! I feel so much better. You're the best," your friend says.

Meanwhile, you settle into your parking spot feeling like you need to bathe in holy water. Your friend pops out of the car and bounces toward the club like a bunny rabbit, not at all aware that they just emotionally vomited all over you without allowing you to get so much as a word in. You take a second and try to collect yourself, but you feel completely drained. If it was up to you, you'd head home right now and just hit the hay.

Has this ever happened to you?

In moments like these, recognize you have just been the victim of what is known as an energy vampire. Energy vampires are sneaky creatures. They come in all shapes, sizes, and disguises. They can often appear as family members, friends, spouses, coworkers, bosses, and even public officials in the news. These energy vampires can strike at any time, sometimes without our even knowing, and it is important to develop a technique and strategy for handling this kind of emotional and energetic overload when it gets thrown at us.

To be clear, these people are not bad people; they are just caught up in dense emotional vibrations—vibrations that we subtly, and sometimes not so subtly, feel. Sometimes the people around us don't know what to do with their frenetic energy other than to literally dump it on someone else. Unfortunately for us, the unsuspecting (and sensitive) bystander, that energy and emotion can often get transferred over, leaving us feeling emotionally zapped while the ranter in chief feels much better having offloaded their baggage. To be fair, we're not always the victims of an energy vampire attack; there's a good chance we behave like an energy vampire ourselves from time to time. Either way, let's discuss how to keep bad vibes from spreading like wildfire and maintain the integrity of our soul force at a basic level.

In an effort to keep our body, mind, and emotions connected to soul force and clear from "stuff" that might get dumped on us unwittingly, I'd like to share a technique I picked up from psychic John Edward. Long ago, I adopted a practice that John calls psychic self-defense, and I have added my own little twist to it over the years. For me, this meditation has been essential in dealing with the energy junk that can get heaped onto me day in and day out. These energy sandbags can get picked up anywhere we have human interaction—especially with those who may be experiencing more dense vibratory emotions like fear, anger, negativity, and jealousy. Basically, grounding to Mother Earth and putting up an energy field of divine light around us allows us be out in the world and sensitive to the energies we engage with, without taking on lower vibrations and carrying them with us. In essence, we're going to visualize energy radiating within and out from us, rather than simply be open to catching whatever energy comes our way.

For me, I've come to refer to this practice as putting up my soul-force field. It is one of the first things I do every single morning when I wake up, and it keeps me more comfortably in tune with my own vibration from the outset of the day. As the next step in awakening our soul force, I want to use this opportunity to not only set up the following exercise but also let you know that the subsequent practices that are going to follow will always begin with a soul-force-field meditation. For the sake of not having to bore you to death by repeating the same protocols over and over, I will prompt you with "Perform a soul-force-field meditation and then . . ." The soul-force-field meditation is the foundation for my daily practice; I use this every morning as well as before I begin to do any kind of energy work, meditating, reflecting, and healing. The reason for this is twofold.

First, I've always felt it is important to have a base practice that is simple and easy to follow and plugs me directly into soul force. Just like athletes start every practice and game with drills that warm up the body and get the senses firing, starting the day with the soul-force-field meditation primes us for consciously interacting with energy—whether it's our own energy or that of the world around us. The more familiar we become with this practice, the more familiar we become with our own baseline soul force, making it more obvious when we are picking up energy that isn't our own. All sturdy houses are built on a strong foundation, and I find the soul-force-field meditation to be sufficient in creating a healthy energetic foundation for maintaining a baseline of energetic integrity.

Second, practicing the soul-force-field meditation on a regular basis allows us to make a consistent and intentional connection to our highest, most expansive, most enlightened self, as well as to our Creator (however we conceive of it) and to the energies of divine light and love. When we engage in our spiritual practice and energy work, we want to connect to only the energy that serves our highest good and the highest good of humanity. Therefore, it is of vital importance to announce our intention to invite the energy of divine white light, love, and our divine Creator—and only this energy—into our spiritual practice.

Now that we've cleared that out of the way, let's dive into the soul-force-field meditation.

Either lying down or sitting in a chair, use rhythmic breathing to turn your attention inward. After you are comfortable and settled into your breathing, call in divine white light, love, and protection by announcing your intention, either out loud or in your mind: "I am connecting to God's divine light, love, and protection."

JEFF BOMBERGER

Please note that you don't have to say God; you can say the universe, the divine, Buddha, Christ, Brahma, source energy, or whatever spiritual language resonates with you in terms of how you conceive of the ultimate life source. If you don't believe in a higher power, simply use the word *love*.

Now imagine a tiny ball of white light on the top of your head. Next, imagine this little white ball rolling down the back of your head, down your neck, and all the way down your spine until it reaches the tip of your tailbone. Imagine the ball connecting to the tip of your tailbone and then unraveling itself into a long white cord that extends downward, like a tail. Now imagine sending this cord down into the core of the earth, until you feel it connect and anchor you to the weight of the earth's gravitational pull. This is your grounding cord. Essentially, this is where any and all negative energy will exit and dispose of itself as it comes to you throughout the day.

Wiggle your toes to become aware of the ground beneath your feet. Then imagine your feet merging with the earth's soil as you grow big thick reddish-brown roots that run deep into the earth. I often envision the roots going deep and then surrounding myself with towering redwoods. I have a real affection for redwood trees and their ancient energy, so I include them in my practice when connecting to Earth's vibration. This is my own way of connecting to the energy and vibration of the planet; you choose something that works best for you. In return, imagine Mother Earth sending you a beautiful, vibrant orange light up through those roots and into your body. Imagine this light as it travels up your legs, into your hips, throughout your torso, along your arms, up your neck, and finally out the top of your head. Feel the warm embrace as this compassionate, nurturing, and creative energy encircles you in a big translucent and protective orange bubble.

Then turn your attention to the sky above. You can imagine any sky—day or night—but I always imagine the deepest indigo night sky above me, shining with twinkling stars. On your own command, part the sky above and envision a luminous white light shining down on you, delivering a powerful energetic charge into the top of your head. As this high vibrational light enters the center of your crown, feel it shoot down through your neck, shoulders, torso, arms, hips, legs, and feet. When the light comes out the bottom of your feet, it expands to form a luminous white bubble of light all around you.

Now imagine yourself inside this bristling field of energy, surrounded by the vibration of heaven and Earth. Sit with these sensations and cycle through a few more rhythmic breaths. Breathe in these high vibrations. Become aware of how this energy feels in every cell of your body, every fiber of your being. Take a moment to release any negative energy down through the grounding cord. You can do this by imagining negative energy taking the form of mud being sucked down into the earth.

Then ask, "Let me be sensitive and aware of the world around me, but only allow the energy that serves my highest good and the will of the divine to stay with me."

Take a few more deep breaths, embracing this protective and revitalizing energy. Sit with that intention to serve the will of the divine, and repeat it as long as you feel necessary. When you feel ready, gently open your eyes and take a few more breaths as you become fully aware and awake in your morning. This is a really simple technique, and it literally only takes a couple of minutes once you get in the routine of practicing and refining the meditation to your needs and liking. For me, it was an excellent habit to get into, and when I finally made the commitment seven years ago to meditate every day, twice a day, this was the first exercise I implemented daily. I like to begin my day with this so that my first interaction with energy is with my own inner voice as well as the light of love and the vibrant energy of Mother Earth. This sets a great energetic tone for me and provides a solid spiritual vibration to take with me into the world.

If you adopt this practice, over time you will become more in tune with soul force. You will also become more

AWAKENING SOUL FORCE

aware of the energy around you as you spend more time in this space. This means that periodically recalibrating throughout the week or even the day can be beneficial in times of high stress and activity. For example, if I know I am going to be doing heavy-duty interacting with people—running a film set with diverse creative personalities or doing healing work with clients—I make it a point to do this exercise before showing up. Life happens, though, and we can't always plan for when our significant other calls needing to vent or a friend or coworker steps into our space and begins to unload all that is going awry in their lives. That's OK; we can clear this energy after the fact with a similar exercise. This can be done with the same meditation above. When you get to the point of being safely in your soul-force energy field, simply imagine releasing any negative energy you're carrying from the day by visualizing it dropping from your body and down the cord into the core of the Earth with every exhale until it clears.

As I became more aware of my own energy and emotional capacities, I began to recognize when I needed to ground myself in a protective energy field throughout the day. For example, on a few occasions, I have been heavily involved in congressional campaigns. Political campaigns are emotional and highly reactive environments. They can be a pretty toxic experience for an empath. Sometimes I'd find myself fielding a frantic phone call and recognizing midconversation that the conversation was emotionally and energetically unwelcome and overwhelming. I'd briefly turn my awareness toward my own soul-force field and spend a few seconds visualizing myself constructing my protective energy bubble so as to mitigate the emotional overload I was experiencing. This allowed me to listen and be present while also creating the energetic and emotional barrier I needed to maintain my wellness.

When an energy-vampire situation arises spontaneously, we also have the power to ask to be excused for just a moment ("bathroom breaks" are great for this) so we can perform a quick visualization for ourselves and prepare for whatever is about to come our way. It's OK to give ourselves the space to energetically be ready to handle emotionally overwhelming conversations. We won't always remember to do this kind of protection in the morning, and sometimes we'll feel the effects throughout the day. The good news is that in addition to the grounding cord I mentioned earlier, we can also use the simple act of washing our hands or using our shower at the end of the day to clear out and cleanse any residual energetic "stuff" we don't want to let sit on us for too long.

The process for this is also pretty basic:

In your mind's eye, visualize your hands and how energetically "dirty" they are. As you begin physically rinsing your hands, imagine the water as the white light of love washing away any dirty or sootlike energy that is stuck to your hands or your body. Imagine watching all those dense vibrations and negative energies be rinsed away in the water and washed down the drain, away from your body and your newly cleared space. Once your hands look clean and clear in your mind's eye, feel free to carry on with your day.

Putting up my own soul-force field and practicing psychic self-defense has been a game-changing practice for me. It has been a key factor in helping me discern my energetic state of being from the rest of the world around me. I encourage you to try this technique for yourself. Give it some time to take root as a personal practice. Be creative and find your own nuances and ways into a safe, protective space that is enjoyable and that resonates in a meaningful way for you. Create rich environments that make you feel joyful and connected. Use imagery that stimulates the sensation of expansion and universal awareness. I can only speak from my own experience when I say that this exercise has been instrumental for my own development, but don't take my word for it. After all, this exchange is about your reclaiming your own soul authority and returning to soul force in your own way.

When you first begin working with this meditation, take a couple of minutes to reflect on or journal about what your initial experiences with this meditation were like. When is it easiest for you to stop and perform this exercise? What does it feel like to connect to Mother Earth? What does it feel like connecting to divine white light, love, and wisdom? What does it feel like to release negative and unwanted emotions through the grounding cord? How does practicing this technique shift your thoughts, feelings, and even bodily sensations? Give yourself some time and space to answer these questions and bring these sensations into your awareness. As we continue along, I hope we're building a whole new language within us, one connected to helping us know and understand our soul force.

CONSCIOUS RELEASE

Becoming aware of energetic or emotional disturbances and learning how to clear them out and let go of that energy is going to be vital for our spiritual health moving forward. Using the grounding-cord release technique has been helpful for me, as has using hand-washing and shower time as a device for consciously washing myself of negative energy. I'd like to introduce another relatively simple technique that can also provide some deeper insight into the energy and emotions we're coming to manage. In this exercise, we are going to use the soul-force-field meditation we previously discussed as the foundation to tune our attention inward.

After you enter rhythmic breathing, drop your grounding cord, and then surround yourself with the protective layer of Heaven and Earth energy, you're going to ask yourself, "What do I most want to let go of today?" An answer will subtly arise to this important reflective question. Often, the answer to this question comes in the form of a negative interaction we had during the day or heavy thoughts, feelings, or even physical pain we're carrying with us. A very specific person may even arise in our mind. What we're going to do is acknowledge this idea, sensation, emotion, pain, person, or experience, and we're going to now consciously release this energy from our energetic, emotional, and physical body.

To do this, you're going to bring your hands out in front of you like you did when I introduced you to the sensation of your soul force. Holding your hands out in front of you about three to six inches apart, I want you to imagine a colored ball of light in between your hands. Once you've created this little ball of energy, you are going to then imagine putting that thought, feeling, person, pain, or experience inside the ball of energy. Run your hands around this ball of light to ensure that whatever you have placed inside is secure and cannot get out. Once you feel like you've sealed whatever it is inside this ball of energy, you are going to take a big deep breath and throw that ball of light up into the night sky and watch it be absorbed by the universe.

Take another deep breath and revel in the sensation of lightness, calm, and relaxation you now feel after you've consciously released this negative energy from your body. Sit with these feelings and sensations for as long as you see fit. Soak in the comfort of having rid yourself of that energetic burden. How does it feel to let that go? Do you notice a difference in your thoughts, feelings, or physical body?

Now you might be wondering, what was up with

AWAKENING SOUL FORCE

the colored ball of light? We use whatever colored ball of light comes to us because it is an indicator of which chakra or energy center we may be working with. We are going to go into deeper detail regarding chakras and the main energy centers in our body later, but for the purposes of understanding this exercise and where we're headed, this is what the color of your energy ball may be indicating for you:

- **Red.** If your energy ball is red, it may be an indication that you are working through matters related to your survival, your home or physical foundation, financial security, and physical safety.

- **Orange.** If your energy ball is orange, it may be an indication that you are working through matters related to creativity, emotions, sexuality, sensuality, joy, and pleasure.

- **Yellow.** If your energy ball is yellow, it may be an indication that you are working through matters related to your public personality, ego, self-confidence, self-worth, and willpower.

- **Green/pink.** If your energy ball is green or pink, it may be an indication that you are working through matters related to the heart, the giving and receiving of love, and intimate personal relationships.

- **Blue/turquoise.** If your energy ball is blue or turquoise, it may be an indication that you are working through matters related to communication, speaking your truth, listening and hearing truth, and spiritual integrity.

- **Indigo/deep blue.** If your energy ball is indigo or deep blue, it may be an indication that you are working through matters related to higher wisdom and intellect, psychic ability, clear vision, and spiritual insight.

- **Violet/white/gold.** If your energy ball is violet, white, or gold, it may be an indication that you are working through matters related to God, the divine, enlightenment, and your highest spiritual connection.

This conscious release exercise is a quick and easy way to tune into ourselves and clear unwanted negative energy and emotions that may be sitting with us. This is also a relatively simple way to engage in a process of self-healing. By releasing the people, places, and things that intuitively feel as if they are weighing us down, we begin to create space to not only feel better but also allow new people, experiences, and emotions to take the place of whatever we released. This process is a small microcosm of the larger spiritual work we will continue to explore and partake in as we move through the rest of

AWAKENING SOUL FORCE

the material. Feel free to build upon, shape, and sculpt this practice in a way that truly resonates for you and helps you recalibrate yourself to your authentic vibration of peace, love, and freedom.

BODY TUNING

Our body is such a vital tool for soul force to communicate and express itself through, which is why I am excited to share with you this body-tuning technique. This exercise is a relatively new practice in my repertoire. A couple of years ago, the wonderful editor of this material, Alicia Lipinski, proposed that I try this as an exercise for getting in touch with my body's own intuition. What I love about body tuning is that I tend to get very clear yes or no answers from the inner knowing of my mind-body connection, rather than get lost in the thoughts of a judgmental, anxious, or cluttered mind. Whether the answer that arises comes from the intelligence of my cells themselves or a more subtle signal from the depths of my energetic self, I can never deny how honest the responses feel when I tap into body tuning.

I'm presenting this exercise as one of the earlier tools we learn to work with, before we get into other mindfulness exercises, because, frankly, as soon as I picked up this technique, I wished I'd had it in my spiritual tool belt all along. It's my own view that this exercise is an excellent step in getting in touch with our own inner wisdom and recognizing that soul force within. Here's how it works:

Start by performing a soul-force-field meditation. After you feel grounded and protected, bring your focus and awareness to your heart space, right in the center of your chest. Take a moment to ease into your deep breathing and really focus on your heart and the chest cavity surrounding it. After a few big deep breaths, ask your body to show you what expansion feels like. With your attention inward, repeat the mantra "Expand, expand, expand . . ." over and over until you feel a very clear sensation arising in your body. While you recite these words deliberately, open yourself up to these feelings and allow them to emerge organically from within. How did that feel? What movements, shifts, or sensations did you notice?

When I first tried the exercise, I sat with the feeling for a moment. I then opened my eyes, shook out my body, reset, and repeated the "expand" mantra again in order to calibrate the sensations and ensure what I was feeling was consistent and clear to me. Again, this exercise is about making a connection to the sensations that want to be expressed through your unique body and how you feel when you consciously focus on expansion.

By turning our conscious attention to expansion and forging a connection with the feelings in our body, we start to build a common language between the soul, the mind, and the body. It's similar to tuning a guitar string. You pluck the chord, listen closely, and slowly turn the tuning peg to find the true harmony of the chord. We can do the same thing with this body-tuning exercise, except we're tuning our conscious awareness to our deepest feelings. For me, expansion is my indicator that I am moving toward something that resonates with my true north—that which intuitively resonates with joy, peace, freedom, growth, and ultimately soul force.

Once you know what expansion feels like, you want to find its opposite: contraction. If expansion is the feeling leading us toward joy, love, peace, freedom, and growth, then we may find it useful to be aware when the body throws us signals that something may be vibrating in the opposite polarity for us. To do this, simply take a couple of deep, conscious breaths and refocus your attention. Clear out the feelings of expansion you were formerly working with by releasing them down your grounding cord. Once you feel reset, settled, and grounded in your body again, turn your attention to your heart space and focus on contraction. Ask your body to show you what contraction feels like and repeat the mantra "Contract, contract, contract..." over and over again until you get a clear sensation in your body. Like before, pay close attention to the sensations that arise. Take a moment to reset and ground yourself, then repeat again.

For me, I get two very distinct sensations in my

chest. When I focus on expansion, my heart feels like it is growing and expanding outward, the way the Grinch's heart grows when all the Whos in Whoville welcome him for Christmas dinner. When I focus on contraction, I get a distinct feeling like the energy and space around my heart is closing and getting smaller—almost like I'm folding in on myself. It feels like watching a pill bug get poked, then recoil and curl up on itself. These are the sensations that arise in me. They may be different for you, which is why it is ultimately up to you to discover for yourself what sensations arise.

It's vital on this journey to move at your own pace and explore the things you feel comfortable and safe exploring on your own. I also want to mention that at this point we are not trying to make big decisions or do anything wildly out of the ordinary using this exercise. The intention of body tuning is for us to simply hone in on how our body tries to communicate expansion and contraction in an intuitive way. We often feel expansion when in the presence of thoughts, words, people, places, and things that are aligned with something true in us. Sensations of contraction may arise in the presence of that which rings false or may even indicate emotional or energetic blockages, which we can decide whether we want to explore further or not. This is not to say that these feelings are the be-all and end-all of intuitive answers on our journey, but for me, they've provided a

AWAKENING SOUL FORCE

wonderful context to be more aware of myself in relation to ideas, people, places, and things.

Now I want to share the second part of this body-tuning technique. It is said that the mind will lie to us, and it is my experience that it can and will lie to us for as long as we let it. The intellect itself has the ability to reason out and rationalize just about anything we can imagine, which is why I've found getting reacquainted with the instincts of the body to be so helpful on this path to self-awareness. I appreciate circumventing the thinking, processing mind as the body can also provide clear insight into our true nature. That's not to say that reason and rationale don't have a place and a purpose in who we are and how we develop, but for the purpose of knowing ourselves and bringing forth that which is true within us, we should aim for the most honest reflection of ourselves possible.

What we are going to do next is ask our body to communicate to us a clear yes and a clear no. This is an extension of the last exercise. Yeses tend to be expansions—those things that are true for us, intuitively drawing us closer to soul force. Nos tend to be contractions—those things that are not true for us or potentially not in alignment with soul force. The setup for this exercise is exactly the same, although I'd recommend standing for this one if you're comfortable doing so. I recommend this because, for myself and other people I've walked through this technique, sometimes the body responds a little more liberally, with an impulse to lean, wiggle, shake, or even take a step. To be clear, I have never seen anyone do this exercise and jump unexpectedly or dart out of the room in some sort of uncontrollable psychic impulse; that's not what we're making space for here. These sensations and movements tend to be very subtle, and I've found it is helpful if you're standing so there can be an unobstructed flow of energy from your crown to your feet. If you can't stand, try sitting up in a chair and paying close attention to how your body responds.

When you're ready for this, take a moment to focus on your rhythmic breathing once again. Draw your attention to the whole of your body. Wiggle your toes and stand firm in your base, aware that you are grounded with the earth. For this technique, I used to close my eyes until I felt movement, but sometimes I perform the exercise with my eyes wide open. Choose whatever is comfortable for you and whatever allows you to focus on the sensations in your body the best. Once you are ready, ask your body to show you what a clear yes feels like. You'll get a sensation. In my case, my hips wiggle a bit. I always repeat this two more times to be sure of what I'm experiencing. Try it again and see what you get. Once you have your answer, move on to the next step.

Next, ask your body to show you what a clear no feels like. Repeat this twice over to be sure of what you're getting as your body's no. Remember, there's no one single way this is supposed to look or feel, so get that idea out of your head. For me, if I ask a question and it's a no response, I feel top-heavy and fall forward. That's how my body responds. As I mentioned before, my yes response is a rather comical slight wiggle in my hips. Your body's response is going to be unique to you. Be open to how your body intuitively reacts, responds, and communicates. Simply ask, receive, let go, and let it flow naturally!

I feel it's worth mentioning to always calibrate and check your yes and no responses if you're going to ask your body direct questions. I say this because your body's method of communication may evolve or change over time. On different days, in different emotional states, and at different times in your life, your body may send different signals. Therefore, always remember to check in and calibrate your body's responses in the present moment before asking your questions. Find your yes and no sensations, then move into questions from there.

Using this technique, we open to trusting the flow of information and energy at an unconscious level. The answers bypass our sometimes-chaotic monkey mind, and our body delivers the message for us. What we each choose to do with that information is a different story, but I do tend to consider these answers as wholeheartedly as I'd entertain any other rational thought I may have. Like

I said, the mind can and will lie to us, especially if it is experiencing fear, anxiety, and lower vibratory states. We owe it to ourselves to allow the higher wisdom embedded deep in our energetic being to also be expressed through our body, not just our mind. The true answers to the questions we seek are always inside of us. For me, this has been true and ever more apparent in the last several years. Body tuning has helped me add another dimension to my approach to solving life's puzzle and remaining in touch with the truth of my inner soul force.

Here are a few questions you can ask yourself for tuning into your body. The answers will obviously vary depending on who and where you are. Make sure you get your clear yes and no signs first, before asking these questions. Ask one question at a time, and feel free to ask it multiple times. Pay particularly close attention to the subtle, intuitive responses.

- Are my eyes brown?
- Am I sitting down?
- Am I indoors?
- Am I cold?
- Did I sleep last night?

How'd these go? What happened? Did you get clear responses? Were they consistent with truth and reality?

AWAKENING SOUL FORCE

Remember, you're simply calibrating here and learning how to listen to and trust your body. To me, it doesn't matter how the responses come about. What matters is that your body is communicating the truth about what *is*. This may seem obvious for easy questions like above, but when we ask more complex and complicated yes or no questions, which can often escape clarity in an anxious mind, we want to have confidence that we can consult our body for more potential insight. When we build up recognition and trust in these intuitive communications, they may grow to hold as much weight as other sensory input we use to make decisions and move through the world. Try these next, more complex questions and see what arises:

- Am I happy at work?
- Do I feel safe and secure?
- Am I creatively fulfilled?
- Do I take on the suffering of others?
- Does my social life serve my highest good?
- Is Jeff totally out-of-his-mind wackadoodle?

OK, I know how that last one probably turned out, so keep that answer to yourself! How about the other questions? Did the responses resonate as true or false?

Did anything surprise you? For this exercise specifically, we're cutting straight to the truth of how our body feels about whatever we ask. We won't dive into the questioning of why you may feel a certain way or not because these are answers you may want to seek on your own, in your own safe space or under the guidance of a therapist or spiritual counselor. I would certainly encourage you to dig deeper into anything you find compelling, interesting, surprising, or unexpected. This work is like peeling back the layers of an onion as the truth of soul force resides deep in the core, beneath all outer layers.

For deeper self-analysis, we can frame some questions in the context of our soul-force foundations:

- Does this thought, person, or activity resonate as true for me?

- Does this thought, person, or activity separate me from soul force?

- Is this thought, person, or activity in alignment with healing?

Finally, this body-tuning exercise may work for some of you. For others, it may not, and that is perfectly OK. There are no shoulds or should-nots on this journey. Walking this path means experimenting with methods that may help you uncover and discover more about what works and does not work for you. If this exercise

AWAKENING SOUL FORCE

resonates and feels like it helps you get more in touch with your true feelings, then wonderful! If not, chalk this up as an experience and move onward! Also, keep in mind that timing is everything. You can come back to this technique at any time in your development and try it again. You may find information flowing more freely and honestly for you at another time. There's no need to get hung up in one spot when we have so much to explore. Let us continue onward and inward!

SOUL-FORCE INVENTORY

To know ourselves truly, we must undo what the world has done to us. The only way to know what has been done to us is to look honestly at our lives—at who we are, what we think, what we believe, and how we act—to see which of those are based on what is true in our heart and soul and which are a result of outside influences. Looking at the sources of these false beliefs, especially painful experiences and past traumas, can sometimes be difficult and scary. Just know that soul force doesn't necessarily need us to retrace painful steps and rehash or relive traumas in order to move forward. Our freedom arises from clearly seeing what is within us and what is outside us and how the two are connected. Unbound by our past, we have the ability to look directly at the here and now, moment to moment, and unlock the answer to the question "Am I in alignment with soul force or not?"

Over the next few moments, days, weeks, months, years—heck, over the course of this whole lifetime—we're going to take inventory of the people, places, things, and experiences in our life that move us closer to or further from soul force. We're looking for expansion versus contraction. We're looking to step into those opportunities to grow into expanded versions of ourselves, and we want to spot those situations that have us trapped in an old version of who we used to be. Using some of the handy tools now found in our spiritual toolbox, we're going to tune out the world, tune into ourselves, and get a good, honest sense of who and what brings us into alignment with soul force and who and what pulls us away from soul force.

There are a couple of ways to take this spiritual inventory:

You can make a literal list in which you go down and use body tuning (or whatever other tools you may have in your practice) to help guide you through this inventory process. Put simply, as you go through the list, you'll use the sensations of expansion and contraction in your body as a measuring stick to give you clarity about which people, places, and things in your life resonate with you . . . and which don't. Start with rhythmic breathing to focus your mind, then gently bring your attention to your heart space and begin to tune into the sensations of expansion and contraction in your body. Perform a body-tuning litmus test to get clear on how your body is communicating today. Once you are confident that you know what clear yeses and nos feel like, go down your list and repeat each name, place, or activity to see if you feel expansion or contraction around each. This is one

AWAKENING SOUL FORCE

way to take spiritual inventory.

You can also become more mindful each day. You may use the soul-force-energy-field meditation to set an intention to be sensitive to the world around you and let the information you receive serve your highest good. This is a much more active process, and it will require more focus, attention, and greater awareness on your part. You'll want to be conscious and aware of the sensations you're feeling in your body when you think about someone or when you interact with them. You'll want to be aware of the sensations in your body when you walk into a particular room or building. You'll want to turn your attention inward toward your heart space as you exercise in the park or throw back a beer after work. The key to this mindfulness is to become aware of what's going on inside and outside you and recognize how they are connected.

A crucial component of this exercise is honesty. Being honest with ourselves means being open to discovering truths we may find inconvenient about ourselves, those around us, and the world at large. When we engage in a process of honest self-reflection, it is inevitably going to rock our world. Engaging fully with this soul-force inventory exercise may very well turn our world upside down. Understand that this is part of the process and that, often, when our true self emerges, it will disrupt our relationship with people, places, activities, and institutions that play a large role in our lives. This is because the agreements and dynamics forged between ourselves and others are based on our history of playing a very specific and particular role in relation to one another.

When we awaken the power of soul force within, these dynamics are inevitably going to shift as we become a more honest, empowered version of ourselves. We shouldn't shy away from this disruption but should instead welcome it as a clear sign that we are moving closer to living out our truth and creating an environment in which we can thrive as a more authentic version of ourselves. This awakening allows us to either reconcile these new revelations within the dynamics we currently experience or choose to move on to new people, places, and activities that resonate more truly for us. Let me share a personal example.

When I was twenty-five, I got married. Nine months later, I was divorced. You're thinking, "Wow, Jeff, I've got bread in the cupboard older than that." It's OK, so do I! Looking back, I recognize I made a huge mistake in entering into that marriage because I didn't enter into it honestly. I don't mean I was cheating or unfaithful; I mean that I rarely embodied and spoke my highest truth in that relationship. So it's no surprise that when I finally did, things imploded. It was as if the commitment to spending my life with this person suddenly turned up the heat in the boiler room, and I recognized that if I didn't start to speak up for myself then, if I didn't start drawing boundaries and working to voice how I was truly feeling, then I was destined for a lifetime of mistreatment and suffering.

For most of our time together, I did a poor job of drawing boundaries. I suffered a tremendous amount of emotional and psychological abuse without adequately sticking up for myself. It'd be easier to blame my ex-wife for her behavior, but I have to own my part in allowing myself to be treated in such a way. By nature, I am a peacekeeper and a caregiver. I want people to feel comfortable, I want people to feel safe, and I want people to feel loved. A part of my personality that was not well developed in this intimate dynamic was the ability to draw hard boundaries and make stern demands about how I wanted to be treated in a romantic relationship. I was living eyeballs deep in what Tibetan Buddhist teacher Rinpoche called "idiot compassion." I was afraid of disrupting the peace, of rocking the boat; therefore, I avoided speaking my deepest truth in an attempt to not make things uncomfortable. In retrospect, I can see that my inability to hold an honest mirror back up to my partner was not an act of compassion but an enabling of her toxic behavior. I wasn't doing either of us a favor.

Eventually, that changed. I started to push back, and I started to shine a light on how I really felt in relationship to her actions. I started drawing boundaries around what I felt was OK and not OK. I stopped cooperating with abusive language and emotional manipulations. After allowing myself and my truth to emerge more honestly, it soon became clear that there was grave divide between us. The more I spoke up and moved into doing what I believed was the right thing, the more psychologically and verbally abusive she became. The stronger I asserted my truth, the more devastating the response. There was a massive spiritual and ethical chasm between us, and it finally became obvious to me this relationship could no longer continue. I had to simply walk away.

This won't be the last time I reference this period in my life as it holds a treasure trove of wisdom related to the journey we're all taking with soul force. The point I want to make with this short summary is this: finding your truth is going to be, on one hand, inconvenient and uncomfortable and, on the other, the best thing that could ever happen to you.

This is the paradox of awakening soul force. I want you to understand this as you embark on the path ahead. Inconvenience is good. Discomfort is good. Where we find inconvenience and discomfort, we find growth and the opportunity to make a new statement about who we really are. We have to be honest with ourselves in this process. If we cannot be honest with ourselves, we have no chance of fully reclaiming our innermost truth and our authentic moral authority. We must be willing to cast aside all illusions and delusions for the sake of what is true. Let's take a quick look at some key areas of life we may want to look at as we recalibrate our alignment with the truth of our soul force.

People

You may have heard the old wisdom that you're the average of the five people you most associate with. While I'd hate to speak in tropes, I'm not afraid to admit when a sound idea resonates, no matter where it comes from. When it comes to your thoughts, your energy, your words, your emotions, and your daily actions, a great place to start is considering the energy and influence of the people you spend the most time with.

Start to pay attention to how your body, mind, and spirit react when you're with someone or meditating on your relationship. A good place to start is with your body. How does this person physically make you feel? Do you feel safe, secure, and energized in their presence? Or do you feel uncomfortable, uneasy, and drained when you're around them? Next, check in on your mind and your thoughts. How does this person influence the way you view yourself and the world? Does this align with the truth about who you really are? Finally, ask yourself on a soul level whether this person intuitively makes you feel expanded or contracted? Do they inspire you to be a better version of yourself, or do they hold you back by keeping you locked in an old image of who you used to be?

Know that there are no right or wrong answers to these inquiries. More often than not, our ebb and flow of energy with people exists on a spectrum and not in absolutes. Remember to not just "think" intellectually about whether these people align with your highest vision of yourself. Do not turn to the mind to see if they check all the boxes because you both like the same movies, shop at the same stores, watch the same television shows, and vote for the same politicians. Those might be expressions of a deeper bond and energetic resonance, but not always. Check in with yourself holistically and feel the resonance of their energy in your body, soul, and mind.

This activity is purely a reconnaissance mission; you aren't necessarily taking any action that would drastically alter the dynamic of your relationship at this point. Right now, simple awareness is our intention. This inventory is about honestly observing, feeling, and acknowledging others with all your senses and checking in with soul force. With that being said, the reality is that a newfound awareness may subtly alter your interactions with people if you begin to notice dynamics that no longer serve you or if there are imbalances in the relationship. Again, we're not going to dive into the specifics of that because

AWAKENING SOUL FORCE

mindfulness and knowing ourselves intimately are most important in this moment.

Look for answers in the same heart space we turned our attention to in the body-tuning exercise. What is it telling you? This process helps us to begin separating the energy, emotions, expectations, and activity of others from our own internal vibration. Make a note of how you feel when in the presence of someone, when you're engaged in dialogue, and when you're apart. These are all key observations that can serve you down the road as you tune into your own soul force.

You can also use the soul-force principles and body tuning to feel out, intuit, and calibrate the personal relationships you hold in your life. Simply turn your attention inward and sit with the following questions:

- Does this person make me feel expansive?
- Does this person inspire the best version of me?
- How is this relationship giving me the opportunity to heal?
- Fundamentally, how does this relationship make me feel?

Answering these questions about the people we surround ourselves with can move us into more honest relationships with ourselves and others. Remember, this is our path to walk, so no one can answer these questions for us. The answers to these questions lie deep within our hearts and at the depths of our soul. By asking questions and seeking the truth, we free ourselves to engage in a much more conscious and loving relationship with those around us and thereby draw us all closer to manifesting soul force in our lives.

Now I want you to take a moment to reflect on this: If you are the average of the five people you spend the most time with, then how much time do you spend with your own authentic self? Are you taking any time to allow this part of yourself to show up in the world and speak to you? In many cases, our family, friends, and coworkers may collectively consume nearly twenty-four out of twenty-four hours of our day on many occasions. If this is the case—that we are constantly surrounded by others and nearly always accompanied by those we share intimate connections with—then when exactly do we get alone time to simply be ourselves and feel free to pursue our own activities and pleasures? Where do we find the time to simply be with our own thoughts, energy, and emotions?

This is not a good or bad value judgment. This is a simple math equation. If our boss and coworkers get us for eight or more hours a day and our family and friends get us for most of those remaining waking hours, where is our time with our own soul vibration? We may even sleep next to our significant other, sharing space in the most vulnerable and intimate way. Honestly, outside of a shower, a meal, or maybe a quick stop at the gym, when do we take time to just be with ourselves? No activity. No desire. No ambition. No hustle. Just time alone with our own emotions, our own energy, and our own soul force so that we can parse through and process our own distinct existence.

My relationship with my ex-wife, which I began to tell you about earlier in this chapter, lasted for about four years. During this particular chapter of my life, my soul force felt uncharacteristically weak and at times distant in my daily experience. For the four years we were together, a lot of what makes me unique and authentically me atrophied and withered away into something not myself. Remember the dreams I said I had in high school about Iraq and the Middle East? That was only the beginning of a phase in which my dream life became incredibly active, reflective, and at times predictive. My dreams played an integral role in my self-development, and I was wholly aware of that—so much so that I kept a dream journal. In it, I would write down any images or messages that felt important, a practice I still do to this day. While I was in this particular relationship, these powerful dreams were few and far between and often times nonexistent. My connection to a deeper part of myself that had once shined a light into darkness in my life seemed to dim to darkness itself.

We'll talk about this in more detail later, but at sixteen, a journaling assignment in English class changed my life. It was that year that I became a writer, and for years after, I journaled often. I journaled deep reflections. I journaled poetry that would spontaneously pour from my soul with incredible ease. It was an integral part of my life. When I was in this former relationship, I journaled much less than normal. I rarely wrote down any reflections, and I rarely wrote poetry. The muse in me was all but silenced for years, intermittently popping into my consciousness, yearning to be acknowledged again, and when I look back on this time period, I can say with full certainty I was unwilling to let the truth within me speak as loud and clear as it used to because I was too afraid of what it might say. I was afraid to acknowledge that this person was no good for me. I was afraid to break the heart of someone whose heart had been broken so many times before. Through conscious ignorance and the suppression of my own feelings and emotions, I bypassed the part of me I'd once known as my highest thought. When I left that relationship, both my dreams and my journaling came back with a tremendous amount of soul force, and I haven't looked back since.

It wasn't until I finally lived alone that I recognized I had fallen into the habit of not affording myself much,

AWAKENING SOUL FORCE

if any, exclusive alone time. For years, my journaling had been that alone time. My meditation had been that alone time. My dream life had been that alone time. So when that time was filled by someone else—someone who was emotionally taxing for me—I fell out of balance. By not taking time to be with my soul force and protect my own well-being, I had also begun to take on more of everyone else's "stuff."

Now, to be fair, the people in our circle who are really in alignment with who we are can be great energy boosts. They are the partners we will move and shake through life with for as long as we're resonating with one another. On the other hand, those people in our lives who pull us away from our center and drag us into melodrama and weighty personal baggage can create quite an emotional and energetic burden—one we have to be able to manage by maintaining a solid grounding in our own soul force.

This is not to say life will always be rosy once we connect with soul force and invite it into our lives. Life happens. People go through things. We will go through growth and healing in order to know our truth more deeply and learn how to live life in alignment with said truth. Part of living with soul force is working through the muck that arises between one another. Part of living with soul force is putting that love and truth into transformative action. Part of living with soul force is experiencing ourselves as what we truly are in relationship to what we are not. We're compassionate beings, so we're going to step up and be supportive and loving when we have the capacity to do so. It's in our nature. However, we have to have the capacity to do so. We have to find our center and be grounded in the strength of our own soul force first. Like they say on every single airline flight, be sure to put on your oxygen mask before you help the person next to you.

From the perspective of energy and vibration, it's important to take the time to tune in to, feel, and understand our own baseline vibration. We have to be in tune with our own frequency so we can be keenly aware of the thoughts, energy, and emotions that originate from our own inner truth rather than from the people around us. After all, it is the light of our inner truth that must radiate powerfully from within, shining a light into the darkness around us, as well as inside us, wherever we go.

Sound

Have you ever heard a song that moved you to tears? Does listening to death metal make you want to thrash your body into a chaotic mosh pit? Do the lyrics to "Bye Bye Bye" take you to a very specific time period? We are all relatively aware of just how powerful sound can be and what a large role it plays in communicating and evoking emotion. We also know that sound is quite literally vibration. Recalibrating the sounds you expose yourself to in your environment can subtly yet powerfully move you more into soul-force alignment.

Turn your attention to the sounds of your environment right in this moment. What do you hear? Busy city streets? The rustle of wind in the trees? Your noisy neighbors? The gentle hum of the refrigerator? Begin to tune in to these sounds and how they make you feel. How do they resonate in your body and in your awareness? You may never have noticed before, but now that we're tuning in, how does that humming of the refrigerator move you? How about those honking horns on the street? What feelings do they inspire in you?

Sound is one of the vibratory senses we're keenly tuned in to but also one we take for granted. Ambient noise, music, and, yes, that TV in the background are all pumping out vibrations and energy, whether we're conscious of it or not. These frequencies have an impact on our thoughts, our emotions, and our energetic state. I believe it is of the utmost importance to become aware of the ambient sounds in our environment because they have so much influence over our life experience at such an unconscious level. As a filmmaker and film lover, I understand this concept and use it intentionally when I place music into a piece. I know that music is vibration that carries its own frequency and tells its own story, which travels from the speakers, through the ear canal, and right into the inner world of the viewer. Artists, musicians, and filmmakers understand the power of sound, and often it's how we move you to feel something without your even knowing it.

Start to pay attention to the sounds of your environment as you move through your day. What sounds do you hear at work, at home, at the bar, at the movies, at the gym, or wherever else you're at? As you tune in to these sounds, check in with your body to get a sense of how you feel in relationship to these audible sensations. Are they disruptive? Are they relaxing? Are they soft and constant? Are they loud and abrasive? Does the music inspire you or make you feel angry? If you have the TV running in the background, tune in to the vibratory frequency of the voice echoing from the screen. Is it pleasant? Does it shriek? Is it low? Is it alarming? Are the words projecting from the TV positive and uplifting? Or is the report negative, violent, or confrontational? Is the tone compassionate, stoic, or aggressive? Check in with all these sensations. If you're listening to music, what kind of music are you listening to and what kind of emotions does it provoke?

Become more conscious of how you interact with sound and music. Take inventory of whether the sounds around you are making you feel connected to soul force or whether they are pulling you out of alignment and into some other vibration. You cannot escape all the dissonant sounds in the universe, but you can become more aware. With this awareness, you reclaim the power to take control of your environment and dial that frequency into a vibration that lifts your spirit, puts you at ease, speaks your emotional truth, and connects you to soul force whenever you see fit.

Believe it or not, I used to listen to nothing but hard metal and grunge rock. To this day, I love to indulge when the mood strikes, but by and large, if I'm doing things around the house, relaxing, writing, or sorting through video footage, I choose to either work in silence or play some ambient instrumental tunes. Classical and jazz are some of my favorite emotionally uplifting tunes to play in the background. I also often resort to solfeggio frequencies, which are sacred chants and ancient spiritual tones I'll use to create deeper spiritual vibes in my environment. Sound plays such an important role in creating a vibration and mood. With this knowledge and awareness, begin to use sound as an emotional and spiritual tool at your disposal. Use sound and music consciously when you can! Accept those you cannot change, and change those you can so that you may utilize sound and audio frequencies to move your vibrations closer to that of soul force.

Check in with our soul-force principles to feel out, intuit, and calibrate your relationship with sound vibrations and music:

- Does this sound/music make me feel expansive?
- Does this sound/music inspire the best version of me?
- How does this sound/music help my own healing?
- Fundamentally, how does this sound/music make me feel?

These questions may seem a little funny at first, but it's a good idea to explore them. When we honor the reality that everything is energy, we can't discount the subtle ways in which sound frequencies and vibrations interact with and manipulate our energy—for better or worse. Reflecting on how sound, music, and musical lyrics resonate inside us can help us become more aware of the vibration we are living in, both consciously and unconsciously. The answer to these questions may sometimes change, like if we're going through a hard time, feeling anxious, or riding a joyful high. Being aware of where we are vibrating can serve as a tool to keeping us in better alignment on an ongoing basis and, ultimately, in a more balanced state.

Media

If you want to do a simple compare-and-contrast on how certain activities intuitively resonate, compare two minutes of blasting reports from the mainstream media news outlets with two minutes of rhythmic breathing to your favorite meditation track. Which one feels better, just imagining the two? Even though I love the art of filmmaking, I watch very little television. I am incredibly selective about the content I consume, both on air and on the web, because there's a reason it's called television programming. When I truly began to pay close attention to the way films, television, and media were making me feel, I had no choice but to make new choices.

As I mentioned earlier, I absolutely love the art of filmmaking. When I set out to create a piece, I understand that I have the power to create an experience for my viewer. Therefore, I very consciously choose how I make my viewer feel. If I'm doing my job right, I am literally crafting a very specific visual, sonic, and emotional vibration and serving it up on a silver screen platter. Remember my words the next time you watch a TV show or movie, listen to a song, or even read a book. Someone—or a whole lot of people, in some art forms—put a lot of very conscious (and sometimes very unconscious) energy into creating content designed to make you feel a particular way. I'll say it again: someone put a lot of very conscious—and sometimes very unconscious—energy into creating content designed *to make you feel* a particular way.

How do your regular television shows and news outlets make you feel? Joyful? Fearful? Happy? Sad? Content? Aggressive? Emotional? Emotionless? Do these projections bring you closer to your highest, purest spiritual truths and ideals, or do they pull you out of alignment? Does this content serve your interests or the interests of those behind the creation?

Flip the script and ask these questions: What do the producers of this show intend I feel by showing me this? What is their motivation for making me feel this way? What is the motivation for telling me this story? For some artists, it is to simply share a feeling, to convey an emotion, to connect with humanity, or to shine a light on a point of view. For others, the goal may be to get something from you—as in your attention, your money, your vote, or your viewership, which then turns into advertising dollars. It is important to question the intention of the content. For those who want something from you other than a chance to move you through their own act of expression and possibly connect on a deeper level, you should scrutinize their creative intentions with razor-sharp awareness.

Take inventory of the media you consume, how you consume it, where you consume it, how much you consume it, and why you choose to consume it. These are all extremely important points of awareness we should strive to familiarize ourselves with. For better or worse, the multimedia we consume has a profound impact on our thoughts, words, energy, emotions, and actions. After binge-watching every episode of *Game of Thrones* in a matter of weeks, I found myself thinking in European accents and wanting to call everyone "milord" and "milady." Our media-viewing habits leave impressions on our psyche. If that weren't true, companies wouldn't spend millions of dollars on Super Bowl ads. If those ads didn't move people to buy things, big business wouldn't spend a penny on advertisements, period. We know visual and sonic impressions can "inspire" people to go out and do things: sign up for a mailing list, buy a car, vote for a candidate. If Facebook ads didn't influence your shopping and voting habits, people with those vested interests would not spend billions of dollars to populate your social media feed with annoying ads that seemingly read your mind.

Advertisers hope these media impressions grab a hold of us so we'll go out and buy what they want us to buy, give money where they want us to give money, and vote for who they want us to vote for. Again, reconsider the phrases *television programming*, *YouTube programming*, and *social media influencers*. What are they programming us to do? How and in whose interests are we being influenced?

Our larger social stories and cultural myths also play a role in shaping our reality. There's a reason tales of heroes elevate and inspire us. In the most well-intended forms, these characters can help us recognize the strength and courage we need to step up and overcome obstacles in our own lives—yeehaw! Yet, to more destructive ends, the stories we consume can also normalize brutal behaviors, foster anger toward one another, and keep us divided and divorced from our unifying soul force.

It's time to take an honest inventory of the media you consume. Sense and feel the vibration your favorite media creators and influencers are operating on. I'm not going to tell you what you should or shouldn't watch or that you can or can't be spiritually aligned and consume a particular kind of content. That is all up to you and how you choose to be in relationship with the material you consume. My point is simply that we cannot pretend the energy generated by TV, movies, Hollywood, PR firms, and our media-savvy politicians exist in some sort of an emotional and energetic vacuum.

Anyone who dabbles in the arts, in marketing, and in psychology knows colors, shapes, sizes, sounds, and images all leave impressions on viewers. Unless we are focused and aware, our emotions are liable to be unconsciously played like a fiddle by masterful artists—sometimes for our highest good and sometimes to keep us divided from ourselves and others. It's up to us, as consumers of content, to decide what we do and do not allow into our energetic space. It is up to us to decide what parts of our nature are going to be fed, nurtured, and cultivated by what we consume. There's a clever parable I really love that I want to share in relation to this particular matter:

An old Cherokee chief was teaching his grandson about life . . .

> *"A fight is going on inside me," he said to the boy. "It is a terrible fight, and it is between two wolves.*
>
> *"One is evil—he is anger, envy, sorrow, regret, greed, arrogance, self-pity, guilt, resentment, inferiority, lies, false pride, superiority, self-doubt, and ego.*
>
> *"The other is good—he is joy, peace, love, hope, serenity, humility, kindness, benevolence, empathy, generosity, truth, compassion, and faith.*
>
> *"This same fight is going on inside you—and inside every other person too."*
>
> *The grandson thought about it for a minute and then asked his grandfather, "Which wolf will win?"*
>
> *The old chief simply replied, "The one you feed."*

While this allegory sums up the journey we're taking as we attempt to awaken and nurture the soul force inside us, I wanted to place the story in this chapter because, as a society today, we spend so much time-consuming media content. In 2016, a Nielsen Company report indicated that the average American spends ten hours and thirty-nine minutes a day consuming various kinds of media, from TV and radio to video on demand and streaming platforms. In 2017, YouTube announced that people spend more than one billion hours watching content on the site per day. Think about that for a moment: if you traveled one billion hours (or roughly 114,000 years) back in time, you'd find yourself at the end of the Ice Age.

Given that we're awakening to this idea that everything is energy and vibration, what kind of state does the content we choose to watch inspire in us? In regards to your consumption of media, which wolf are you feeding?

Employing soul-force principles can help you tune in, intuit, and calibrate your media consumption. Try asking yourself these questions when engaged with the news, television, film, advertisements, and digital content:

- Does this program make me feel expansive?
- Does this program inspire the best version of me?
- How does this influencer help my own healing?
- Fundamentally, how does this content make me feel?

Like anyone else, I am a sucker for good, well-written drama and fantastical stories. With that said, we want to be conscious of the amount of heavy and dense emotional vibrations we expose ourselves to, especially if we're moving through our own challenging situations in real life. Mustering the power, will, and energy to work through our relationships, our wounds, and our trauma is a heavy lift enough all by itself! We may want to consider avoiding drowning ourselves in too much drama by "escaping" into more hardcore drama.

Remember the point I made earlier about the five people you spend the most time with? Let's say a person in a toxic situation finds themselves surrounded by a verbally abusive boss, a controlling boyfriend, a spoiled dog . . . and Walter White on Netflix. In terms of energy and emotion, what kind of vibration is being reinforced here, over and over and over? Is this media consumption healthy for our sample person, especially given these imagined circumstances?

Start to think of consuming media the way you would approach inviting people into your home. Energetically, you're doing the same thing by plopping in front of the television or lying in bed with your iPad. The world can be a dark and scary place, and our media often like to reflect that. Yet the world is also a vibrant and magical place.

Much of our modern experience and the technology that has enhanced and extended our lives was once merely the work of science fiction's most creative and imaginative minds. In essence, our spiritual trajectory has more in common with the expansive world of Disney and the magical wonder of Harry Potter than it does with action flicks and hardcore human drama — not because violence and trauma aren't aspects of our human condition, but because our spiritual condition beckons us to the possibilities of what we could be in our highest image.

Knowing what we are and who we've been is important on this quest to seek truth, yet so is being open to the vision of what we may become. The media we consume, the stories we absorb, and the characters we invite into our lives can either suppress or enhance that ideal vision. Which wolf we feed is entirely up to us.

Diet and Fitness

I spent over ten years working as a personal trainer, so truthfully, I feel like I could write an entire book on this subject alone. Simply put, organic, natural, nutrient-rich, and high-vibrational foods, along with moving your body in an enjoyable, sweat-inducing way, are integral to maximizing soul force. In my humble opinion, a healthy body helps propel us through the spiritual work we are called to do in this lifetime and gives us the physical strength, energy, and stamina to move through this extremely dense material existence gracefully and effectively.

Illness and various forms of disease are a part of life, and we'll all be called to wrestle these challenges and heal them when they arise for us. With that said, I do feel strongly that maintaining a healthy body, as a clean and clear channel for soul-force energy, can improve our ability and power to manifest, create, and sustain ourselves on this journey. In fact, if you're an athlete, a martial artist, a dancer, or a performer of some kind, your physical body is quite prominently at the center of your soul-force expression!

One of the things I came to realize over years of helping people transform their lifestyles through diet and fitness is that there is no one-size-fits-all solution. While there is incredibly deep and detailed science that can guide us to achieving very specialized and specific fitness goals, some fitness regimens and nutrition programs work for some people and not for others. Bodies are different. Genetics vary. Mind-sets and preferences are unique to each person. Decades of prior lifestyle, diet, and other choices factor into the health, vitality, and metabolic balance of our bodies.

Having a healthy body is also more than just looking good. Adequate flexibility, joint range of motion, and healthy, hydrated tissues are all aspects of wellness to consider outside of looking cute naked. We also need to consider how much we enjoy the activities we participate in and what food fuels our bodies best.

When I started out as a trainer, I used to come in with all my research, stats, and perfectly calculated regimens, and I'd try to impose them on all my clients because science says "this" is what works. Yet what I discovered over time was that the more I blended hard science with approaches that intuitively resonated with my clients, the more sustainable their lifestyle changes would be. Often, with this approach, they would enjoy greater gains in their overall fitness and wellness because it was balanced with the things they enjoyed and were drawn to. After all, movement can be a deep expression of our soul force if we allow it.

Just like in other areas of our lives, when it comes to having a healthy body, balance is key. For example, if a client absolutely hated lifting weights, I would design a program that maximized the benefits of weight training but minimized the amount of time spent on it; that way, they could enjoy the workouts while still getting the proper work the body needed to become healthier. If someone said they were unwilling to eat organic foods, I could craft a meal plan that maximized the nutritional benefit of the food they did eat while introducing healthier, alternative meal choices every so often so the client could slowly introduce new approaches to their diet. I always asked clients to be brutally honest about what they liked and didn't like, what made them feel great, and what did not. Like the rest of the journey we're on now together, the truth always sets us free.

Take an honest look at your diet, your physical activity, and your lifestyle. What activities make you feel energized, healthy, and vibrant? What ways of moving your body do you most enjoy? Sports? Hiking? Gardening? Dancing? What foods make you crash? Which foods give you sustainable energy boosts? Which meals leave you feeling bogged down and lethargic? Which ones give you strength?

It's important to also evaluate your emotional relationship with food and exercise. Do you eat when you are feeling sad? How about when you're angry? How do those foods seem to settle when you eat them in those moods? Do certain foods give you a sense of comfort or deep nourishment? Do any make you happy or remind you of favorite memories? What activities help you blow off steam? Which lift your mood?

Let some of these inquiries be the starting point from which you can begin to work on and shape a healthy and balanced lifestyle plan for yourself. Whatever activities boost your vitality, do them! Whatever foods give you sustainable energy and nourish your body, eat them! It really can be that simple if we allow it to be. Yet first, we have to understand where we are right now. We are embarking on an intuitive discovery of our inner self; whatever our inquiries reveal and whatever truths we discover will provide the foundation from which we can adjust our total spiritual, mental, emotional, and physical alignment. Take time to slowly unravel yourself so that you may allow your soul force to guide your lifestyle choices.

Check in with our soul-force principles to intuit, feel out, and calibrate how your lifestyle choices are resonating with your highest self:

- Does this exercise routine / food make me feel powerful?
- Does this routine/food inspire the best version of me?
- Is this routine/food healing for my body?
- Fundamentally, how does this routine/food make my body feel?

Hippocrates famously said, "Let food be thy medicine." A healthy diet, coupled with physical movement, can lead to transformative healing all on its own. The food we eat carries vibration and energy, just like everything else. Calories are literally a measure of how much energy is packed into a gram of carbohydrate, protein, and fat. The calories we consume through food and expend in movement are unique in that we can see, touch, taste, smell, and feel the results of this energy exchange in the wellness of our physical body. One of the ways we can maximize soul force is by practicing diligent self-love and care of our physical body. It is, after all, the only vehicle we get to drive on this wild journey this time around. The body is a bridge between our inner world and our shared reality. Therefore, it is important to keep the body healthy and strong so it matches the dynamic power of our soul force within.

Reflecting Back

Make sure that as you move through this process of taking inventory in these different areas of your life, you take time to reflect on your discoveries. It's a good idea to start a journal and put your observations on paper. Committing to a journaling practice at the end of each day can help serve as a reminder to pay attention to your surroundings and become more aware of how you feel. It can also help you to process the discoveries you make along the way. Some simple journal prompts for the end of the day could include the following:

- When did I honor my truth today?
- When did I betray my truth today?
- How did it feel to honor my truth today?
- How did it feel to betray my truth today?

EVERYTHING IS ENERGY

We are awakening. Becoming more mindful of our own intuition is awakening. Becoming more mindful of our thoughts is awakening. Becoming more mindful of our emotions is awakening. Becoming more mindful of our physical being is awakening. Becoming more mindful of how we feel in relationship to our environment is awakening. In order to free ourselves from what the world has impressed upon us, we must become more aware of the true sensations that arise in us. In order to free ourselves from the chains of bondage we have placed on ourselves, we must become more aware of ourselves and the world around us. A crucial understanding in this great awakening is this:

Everything is energy

All thought, word, action, and matter are energy. This fundamental concept is going to inform everything we do and discuss from here on out. The "material" existence with which we interact with every single day is pure energy. Everything from the seen to the unseen in this universe carries its own unique vibratory frequency, including us, and it is all constantly in relationship. Quantum physics tells us that everything is, quite literally, energy and that this energy is constantly moving and vibrating. The laws of physics and chemistry tell us energy cannot be created nor destroyed; it can only transform or be transferred from one form to another. To truly understand this, we need to get beyond the intellect of the mind and begin to turn our awareness toward the multitude of ways in which we sense and emit these vibrations intuitively. It was Nikola Tesla who said, "If you want to know the secrets of the universe, think in terms of energy, frequency and vibration."

We don't have to be quantum physicists to understand this concept at a level that is relevant and impactful to us. Let's say you and I are enjoying a lovely hike in Yellowstone National Park. We're surrounded by gorgeous nature, crisp blue skies, and tons of impressive natural wildlife scurrying about. We stop for a water break in the middle of our hike, and suddenly my eyes grow wide as I yell, "There's a bear behind you!" You're immediately sent into a panic. Sensing danger, your neurons fire, neurotransmitters are released, and your sympathetic nervous system kicks you into fight-or-flight mode within nanoseconds. The hormone cortisol is released to deliver energy and nutrients to your muscles, your heart rate rises, and you begin perspiring, ready for a fight. You whip your head around, eyes wide open, ready to grapple to the death, only to discover there is no bear.

Amused by your reaction, I begin to laugh hysterically. All sorts of biochemical reactions follow and neurotransmitters flow, making me feel light and joyful, as uncontrollable belly laughter erupts from my body. You, on the other hand, don't find the whole situation so funny. Your fear turns into anger, and you physically swat me on my shoulder to display your displeasure with the whole situation. Suddenly, my lightness and joy are squashed by the residual sting of your smack to my shoulder. As we continue on our hike, you hold on to a lingering fear that a bear might show up. You weren't scared at all before, but now that I planted that idea in your mind, you can't seem to shake the possibility from your mind. As I continue on the hike, I refrain from any further practical jokes that may spook you enough to give me a good whack again. Suddenly, our once lovely, carefree hike is tainted by a subtle tension that all began with what I thought was a funny joke.

I use this example because it is going to serve us well on many levels moving forward. First, it illustrates how powerful words, sound, and vibration can be. There is good reason the sages have reminded us to be, as author Don Miguel Ruiz Jr. says, impeccable with our word. Our word is energy, and it has the power to literally create our reality. In our short example above, look at the ripple effect that my words had. Even though my intention was to be funny, my words weren't aligned with truth because there was no actual bear. Instead of inspiring laughter, they created fear, anger, a small amount of shoulder pain, and a lingering tension between friends. Which brings me to my next point.

This example illustrates how our senses can be deceived and manipulated yet still create a very real and palpable lived experience. Even though there was no bear, you still experienced panic. Even though there was no bear, your heart rate jumped. Even though there was no real danger of harm, I ended up with a sore shoulder. Even though there was no bear and my intention was to joke with you, you're now carrying a fear that a bear may appear at any moment and devour us, which is infringing on your joy. I began the hike with no pain in my shoulder, but because of the energy I set in motion, now my shoulder is a little sore. For both of us, the only remedy at this point is to be honest, acknowledge the truth, and heal from this moderate discord that was created. Understanding that everything is energy—including thoughts, words, and other subtle vibrations—is going to be key to tuning our vibration to that of soul force as we move forward.

Finally, our imagined interaction in Yellowstone demonstrates the continuous and unbroken chain of cause and effect that drives our experience. Energy cannot be created nor destroyed; it can only transform or be transferred. The joy we shared on the hike was transformed when I had the thought that it would be funny to give you a bear scare. The energy of that thought gave rise to the energy I projected out of my mouth, which was transferred to you via my word. When the vibration of my yell was decoded by your brain, my word became your thoughts. This mental energy gave rise to electrical impulses that activated a chain of biological responses within your body as the energy of your thought was transferred and transformed into neurological energy. This neurological energy became physical movement when your eyes opened wide, your heart raced, and your body spun around in a panic. So, as you can see, it was my own energy that eventually came back around and smacked me in the shoulder. How's that for quick lesson on karma?

Do you see the power of the energy exchange we share in every moment of every day? Do you see the subtle and not-so-subtle way in which we experience, share, create, receive, transfer, and transform energy, without end? Do you see how being aware of this process can transform the way we live our lives? Can you think of an example in your life when thoughts became words, words became actions, and those actions became something you had never experienced? Can you think of an experience you had that created a particular perception in you that then impacted future experiences? For example, let's say that you were never able to let go of the thought that a bear might attack you after my silly prank, and now every time you go hiking, there's always a hint of fear percolating under the surface of your emotions. Can you see how a simple untruth can rob us of the truth of our own experience? Can you see the power of being able to let go of these untruths and accept the truth of experience? Can you see why we must become aware that everything is energy if we are to be free?

We are hardwired to be energy-sensitive beings. Think of all the stimuli we process every day, from the emotional state of a loved one to sound waves oscillating in our ear pods. Have you ever recognized your partner was angry by simply stepping into the room with them? This is the simple power of vibration and frequency in our tangible experience. Some of us not only sense the emotions and energy of others but can also *feel* them, even if we don't want to. This is because we are equipped, through trillions of cells, to be sensitive to subtle vibrations, and that energy can be transferred to us through the vibration of thoughts, emotions, words, and, in the most material form, physical action or force. In turn, our own personal vibration, as well as the quality of our thoughts, feelings, words, and actions, impacts not just us but the greater world around us. Now, for the purpose of this discovery process—the soul work we're responsible for—I want us to open up to our own subtle senses and begin to really explore the vibrations we feel, sense, and ultimately create for ourselves.

For now, I want you to turn your attention to the sounds you can hear in the background while you read this book, right now in this instance. How do they strike your ear? How many sounds are there? How do they make you feel? Sit with that for a moment. Then, when you're done, look at the image on the front cover of this book. Draw your attention to the color, the framing, and the composition. What's your general sense? What impression do you get? What emotion do you feel? Now turn your attention to the center of your chest as you read the following words:

I am love incarnate. I am connected to the divine. I am soul force.

How did reading those words feel? How did they move you? Let this mindfulness process become second nature as we move through this material and move out into the world. Periodically check in with your senses, with your heart, with your gut, and with how you ultimately feel. Becoming keenly aware of these sensations is going to be key in finding our direct connection to soul force and unlocking the healing and transformation that await us on this journey.

Everything has its own unique vibration in this universe, including us, as we've discovered. It wasn't until I began living in my own apartment, without anyone around, that I began to become emotionally, energetically, and consciously in tune with my own vibration. There were no friends around wanting to party, no parents buzzing in and out, no significant other vying for attention. When I wanted to be alone, I was alone. When I afforded myself this opportunity to be completely alone in my own space, disconnected from the energy and vibration of other people, I began to truly get in touch with my own personal vibration. It's almost embarrassing for me to admit that I truly didn't feel or fully recognize my own vibration until I was nearly twenty-six years old. For a quarter of a century, I wrestled with complex feelings and emotions I could not necessarily claim or explain because I honestly didn't know what the heck they were all about. I had never given myself the space or the permission to get to know myself outside of my relationship with everything else. Think about how confusing that really is. How is it even possible to be in any kind of conscious relationship to anything in the world without knowing who we are first?

I was definitely aware that some people made me "feel" better than others. With some folks, I could engage in conversation and come away wanting to chat forever because the interaction was so energizing. With others, I'd be looking for a dark closet to run and hide in after a few brief moments of interaction; these people, who you and I now recognize as energy vampires, would feel to me physically dense with energy and emotions. At an instinctual, even intuitive level, I was aware of these sensations.

I was also aware that some strenuous activities actually gave me energy, while less physically taxing endeavors would sometimes drain more life from me than I would have expected. For example, I feel better after eight hours of manual labor than I do if I have to spend eight hours looking at a spreadsheet. Moving my body, breaking a little sweat, and physically expending energy actually leaves me feeling more energized at the end of the day than if I were sitting in a cozy office, sipping tea, and crunching numbers. If I'm stuck working solely on budgets and spreadsheets, time drags. By the end of the day, I feel like my body has been filled with cement, and I crave physical movement. I think it's therefore safe to say that being an accountant would not be a soul-force-aligned career choice for me. You, on the other hand, may be someone who absolutely loves working with numbers and organizing things in spreadsheets, whereas a fifteen-minute jog wipes out your energy for the day. That's what's kind of cool about us all being different. These realities aren't inherently good or bad; they just are. It's up to us to pay close attention to our energy levels and be conscious of what makes us come alive, because that's what we're meant to be and bring into the world, both for ourselves and others.

Until I began the search for answers about who and what I really was at my core, I didn't really know who, what, or why I was feeling what I was feeling most of the time. That changed when I was finally out living on my own. To be clear, living and being alone didn't immediately make my world Candyland. In fact, for the first few weeks, there was a tremendous amount of fear, anxiety, and loneliness that set in. I became acutely aware that there was no one around to share life with—a comfort I'd enjoyed for a quarter century. It felt really foreign at first. I had no one to discuss current events with at home. Late at night, I missed laughing at the television with someone close to me. I quickly recognized that I was attached to the presence of others. I wouldn't go as far as to say I was fully dependent, but there was definitely a semblance of dependency and normalcy around sharing space with someone else. I realized that this was something I needed to take a good, hard look at if I wanted to grow as an individual person.

After those initial feelings of isolation and loneliness came to pass, I found myself having dramatic mood swings and fluctuating emotions. I would have streaks of days where I felt like I was this unstoppable force capable of anything and everything. I would be energized by the prospect of life and all its beauty, wonder, and opportunity and . . . squirrel! My mind was all over the place. I wanted to write. I wanted to train clients; I wanted to do more acting. I wanted to move to another city. Every once in a while, I'd hit a remarkable crash and slip into what I would later identify classify as bouts of mild depression. I would feel unmotivated, cynical, angry, and irritable. I didn't want to go out and socialize. Even the most mundane tasks seemed incredibly difficult to complete or even bother with. In all, some days my soul force would feel incredibly strong, and on other days my soul force would feel completely depleted.

It was at this point in my journey that I decided to take the whole "everything is energy" axiom more seriously, so I started to look at my environment. I read a book by Dr. Bruce Lipton called *The Biology of Belief.* Thanks to Dr. Lipton's work, I began to look quite attentively at all things in my immediate experience. The book enlightened me on the field of epigenetics, which is the study of how our environment affects our gene activity and expression. This book opened my eyes to the simple fact that, in a strictly biological sense, we are a collection of trillions of intelligent single cells, acting and reacting at a cellular, instinctual, unconscious level to every single bit of stimuli we're exposed to. Our thoughts are influenced by the energy input into us through our perception of the world. These internal perceptions give rise to the mental and emotional energy we know as thoughts and feelings, which then inspire the body to take particular action.

If the sounds I hear, thoughts I think, words I speak, experiences I have, and food I eat can truly alter what my biology is doing or not doing without my being conscious of it, I figured I'd better get to being more self-aware. I couldn't help but wonder what I'd feel like if I sought to be more purposeful in how I crafted my environment. What if I was more thoughtful about creating as much harmony around me as I possibly could? Would this impact me at all? I wondered what would happen if I paid closer attention to what I was exposing myself to at every level of existence. How would I feel? Would my emotions stabilize? Could I somehow reset the baseline of my own vibration and feel clearer by simply immersing myself in an environment that intuitively resonated with my own soul force? And if I could, how would I know it was right?

I worked quite a bit as an actor as a child, both in television and commercials, and then again as an adult. Actors at their core are emotional instruments. Just as guitar strings wail notes and bass drums thunder beats, actors are merchants of emotion and energy. They embody the whole spectrum of human experience: happiness, sadness, joy, betrayal, ambition, despair. When we watch gifted actors on the stage or the screen, we feel these emotional states emanating from them, and we begin to relate to them—to form a bond through our shared humanity. Their experience becomes our experience. After a little reflection, I realized that this emotional exchange doesn't stop just because a camera stops rolling, so I slowly began tuning into my emotional state, like an actor would, all the time. I became more aware of how I was taking on and wielding energy in the world.

Instead of imagining myself as a singular point of view trapped inside my skull, having an intellectual experience of a world outside me, I began to consciously regard my entire body as a bridge between the world inside and outside myself. I stepped into honoring the full, direct experience of life flowing in and out of me. I opened myself up to the natural ebb and flow of emotional and energetic vibration between inner life and outer life. I embraced this idea that the inner and outer world are not separate but one and the same. The truth is, if we're alive and breathing, then this interconnected exchange of energy between inner and outer reality is constant, whether we are aware of it or not. We have to realize that this is true for all of us. It is this self-awareness that is going to be pivotal for our transformation on this journey.

If you've ever been moved by an actor's performance, you've experienced this emotional and energetic transference for yourself. Life is a constant transaction of energy, like money changing hands. It's the real deal! Maybe you've never thought of it this way, but that is exactly what is taking place. Our body takes in experiences, which we can consider as energy deposits into our energetic bubble. We also expend energy, which can be considered as withdrawals that flow outward from our energy bubble and in the direction of the world outside of us. For a guy who hates spreadsheets and budgets, thinking of the dynamic energy exchange in this way really shifted my experience. As soon as I accepted this notion that I am emotionally and energetically communicating with the world around me and that the world is communicating back to me, both consciously and unconsciously, at all times, I found a key to bringing myself into alignment with soul force.

The gift of this revelation was that I no longer wondered if who I was with, what I was doing, where I was doing it, and why I was doing it was affecting my body, soul, and mind. There was no longer any question at all. I fully acknowledged that it was 100 percent connected to my overall well-being as well as my own clear sense of self. With this new awareness, I began to engage in the rigorous process of self and environmental scrutiny. I knew that, with effort and awareness, I could tune my vibration to a frequency that was most reflective of my highest spiritual values and ideals. Most importantly, I sought to align myself with what is true—both objectively to the outside world and internally within me.

Understanding that, fundamentally, all of life is a natural flow—an effortless and intuitive give-and-take of energy—is crucial to our spiritual alignment. What we seek on this path is a true vibration, a harmonized resonance, and a pure connection to soul force. In this exploration, we aim to find ways to distinguish between what energy subtly springs forth from within us as a true expression of our connection with soul force and what energy and vibrations we've soaked up from the world outside us, which we may be holding on to inside of us. As we will learn in the next chapter, keeping energy gracefully flowing back and forth between ourselves in the world is vital to realizing true soul force for ourselves.

INTRODUCTION TO CHAKRAS

So far, you and I have been exploring a deeper awareness of our mind and body as they relate to our environment. We've also started to explore how everything is energy and the impact that our own energy has on our daily lives. Now it's time to explore our subtle energy body and our intuition in a more intimate way by working with what is known as our chakra system. *Chakra* is the Sanskrit word for "wheel," which is appropriate because chakras are energy centers through which soul-force energy spins and flows. These wheels of energy run up the median of the body, from the tip of our tailbone to the crown of our head, in vertical alignment with our spine. The chakras each have a corresponding color on the spectrum of light, with the colors working their way up in vibratory frequency: red, orange, yellow, green, turquoise, indigo, and violet.

These invisible, rechargeable spinning wheels of energy share a relationship to different aspects of ourselves on a spiritual, mental, emotional, and physical level. Our chakras can be broken up into "higher" and "lower" chakras (but please keep in mind that this is not meant to imply a hierarchy). The first three chakras—the root, the sacral, and the solar plexus chakras—have to do with our more physical, base, earthly needs and connections. The fourth chakra, our heart chakra, is the bridge between these lower chakras and our higher chakras—the throat, the third-eye, and the crown chakras—which are related to our spiritual aspirations, higher ideals, and connection to the divine.

We'll go into depth on each of these in a moment, but, in brief, the first chakra, the root chakra, is related to our basic survival. The second chakra, the sacral chakra, is connected to emotions, creativity, and joy. The third chakra, the solar plexus chakra, is related to our identity and willpower. The fourth chakra, the heart chakra, corresponds with matters of love and healing. The fifth chakra, the throat chakra, is related to truth and communication. The sixth chakra, the third-eye chakra, is connected to intuition and higher wisdom. Finally, the seventh chakra, the crown chakra, is our direct link to our divine source of creation.

The chakra system is considered the backbone of our spiritual integrity, much in the way that our spinal column keeps our skeletal body upright and aligned. Our chakra system maintains the integrity of the mind, body, and spirit as an entire system by keeping our holistic selves upright, so to speak. We can think of taking on chakra work as becoming our own energy chiropractors, spending time and attention balancing and aligning these centers. When we balance these chakras, we allow soul force to be more freely expressed through our body and mind. The chakra system is a road map we can use for maintaining our holistic wellness, as it gives us clear signs and reference points for where we may need more balance and healing. By developing a basic understanding of these energy centers, as well as the spiritual, emotional, and physical attributes they're connected to, we may spot imbalances, fix problems, heal wounds, and unleash new potential within ourselves.

Remember all my raving about how excited I was when I realized energy was constantly flowing from life into me and from me back out to life? The chakra system organizes and regulates that energy for us and allows us to be more aware of the energetic exchange taking place, as well as its effects on our mind, body, and spirit. Think of the chakras as energy gateways that allow energy to flow in and out, between ourselves and the world. In this way, our inner reality and our outer experience are intimately connected by this system. It is important to ensure that energy passes in and out of these gateways freely. Energy will always be on the move, and it wants to flow. When there is an obstruction of flow, our energy can get clogged, backing up the system until the energy either spills over or comes to a stagnant standstill. It is therefore important that we do our best to prevent these energy blockages, keep each chakra from becoming overactive or underactive, and ultimately keep the whole system in harmonious balance.

Energy blockages can develop where we hold on to trauma, illusions, negative experiences, suppressed emotions, damaging thoughts, and self-limiting beliefs that do not serve our highest good. Like a Brita water filter, sometimes our chakras can get clogged up with this energetic "gunk." If we don't go inward and intuitively work with our chakras to see what's stuck and clean the filter, this blockage may then manifest itself as unpleasant thoughts, emotional turmoil, and even physical pain. Since we're dealing with the energy that is cycling between ourselves and the world, blockages create energy insufficiencies. Let's say you had domineering parents and it was difficult to speak up from a very young age. Because this truth-speaking energy was suppressed, that could lead to your experiencing underactive or insufficient energy in the throat chakra, the center connected to communication. Or let's say you hold the belief that life is a constant struggle. This belief could then act like a dam, blocking you from experiencing abundance, safety, and security, even when it walks right into your life. Underactivity in a chakra center can not only keep us from being open to new energy and experiences flowing into the center, but it may also keep us from being able to adequately express new energy outward.

AWAKENING SOUL FORCE

For example, in a breath work session I did, I began to experience a tingling in my right hand and all the way up my arm about fifteen minutes into the session. As I dove into what was causing this, I found an energy blockage in my heart chakra. The heart physically rules the hands and arms, so the blockage ended up manifesting itself as a tingling sensation in these parts of my body. This blockage, in particular, was related to a lot of deep emotional pain I was feeling that was related to betrayal in personal relationships. I had just moved through a string of experiences with my heart wide open where it felt like my sincerity and kindness was taken advantage of. This began to take its toll, both energetically and emotionally, and slowly my abundance of love was becoming a bit inaccessible with certain people. It wasn't until I consciously moved into that energy center to work with this blockage that the sensation dissipated and I was able to clear new space to reconcile tensions in those relationships. Part of the ongoing work that came out of that session was developing a strategy for not allowing myself to get taken advantage of energetically and emotionally in the future. This was crucial for bringing my heart center back into balance. Later, as we move through each of the seven energy centers, I will be sharing mental, emotional, and physical strategies that allow us to power up an underactive chakra when we need to.

JEFF BOMBERGER

When it comes to balancing chakras, a lot of focus tends to get placed on energy blockages that dissipate energy, but our chakras can experience a state of being overactive and flowing with too much energy as well, like a powerful light that is drawing too much electricity from the grid. Having too much energy in one or a number of centers also throws us off balance. For example, if you have hyperactivity in the third-eye and crown chakras but your root chakra is severely underactive, then you are not as energetically grounded as you could be. You may find yourself aloof, spacey, or deeply immersed in the ethereal realms while lacking an ability to bring that spirituality into practical, living, breathing existence. You may be a bit out of touch with reality and need to develop a strategy to be more present in your body and the world around you. Conversely, you could be experiencing an overabundance of root-chakra energy, which may make you physically aggressive or even violent in your attempts to feel safe and secure in the world.

As I mentioned earlier, energy wants to flow and move freely; therefore, a blockage can also create an overabundance of flow if the energy is being directed in ways that do not align with soul force. Another example from my own experience is that when I am not creatively expressing my own inspirations, my sacral chakra can go into hyperdrive. I spend a lot of time creating content with other people, and I've found that if my creative energy is being directed only into these collaborations and I'm not writing and creating my own content, I get extremely restless. Suddenly, I'll have this impulse to start a million projects of my own—books, scripts, movies, and music. I've come to recognize this as a sign to myself that I need to create something of, by, and for myself. When I'm not creating for my own sheer joy, my sex drive also tends to kick into high gear (as this is also connected to the second chakra), and there arises a general sense of unease and restlessness that indicates that my creative energy needs to be redirected into something more soul satisfying. Thanks to studying the chakra system and doing this work, I have learned how to more quickly identify and correct these energy imbalances. I'll be discussing how you can bring your own energy centers back into balance in the pages ahead.

We're going to focus on the seven main chakras in this introduction to the chakra system. Ultimately, we want to see if we can work on clearing, maintaining, and balancing these energy centers ourselves as much as possible. Physical trauma and lived experiences can leave lasting impressions on our chakra centers, especially if we've never done any conscious healing work before. These experiences from the past can resurface and emerge into our conscious awareness when we begin working within each energy center. Therefore, it is important to be patient, kind, and loving toward yourself as you begin to reconcile these aspects of yourself.

The energetic footprint of past experiences, as well as adopted beliefs, psychological conditioning, and social constructs, can remain with us even when they no longer serve us. If we hold wounds embedded deep in our psyche, then it isn't until we revisit these tender spots with loving awareness that we can let them go and transform this energy for good. This is why it is essential to confront our past pains and traumas nonjudgmentally, to look at the lessons and the growth we can take from them, and to then discard them and let them go. This process will take courage. The journey will require forgiveness. Healing will take time and effort. When we sincerely do this deep inner work, we clear space for new experiences to enter our lives and to allow our true selves to emerge more firmly in alignment with soul force.

There is no expectation for us to do this work completely alone, although we may if we so choose. Working with trauma or blockages related to abandonment, abuse, oppression, suppression, fear, betrayal, anxiety, insecurity, violence, physical pain, emotional manipulation, and economic violence can all seem frightening. God has given us all the power we need to overcome these challenges, and our soul force will help guide us through this process. While we are here to reclaim our soul authority and realize the healing power of loving awareness within, this also means we get to choose who we partner with and who we move through our healing with on this journey. Ultimately, it is up to us to decide when and where we may seek support, guidance, and outside assistance to help us realize pure soul force. As the saying goes, when the student is ready, the teacher appears. That teacher could take many forms: your doctor or therapist, a coach or mentor, a friend or family member, your banker or grocer, the person who changes the oil in your car, or a person experiencing homelessness holding a sign on the corner of the street. We are all gifted healers in our own way, and we should keep our hearts open to the guidance that feels right when it appears. Follow your intuition, and allow your instincts to guide you in your healing process.

ROOT CHAKRA

Survival of the fittest. Do or die. Kill or be killed. Get a piece of the pie. When it comes to our cultural programming, the belief that there is not enough—that life is a competition—is fundamental in many of our cultural stories. If we look at this deeply, we see an unconscious belief about our world that immediately pulls us out of energetic balance at our most fundamental level. When we look out into our world, we see competition everywhere: in school, in sports, in business, in politics, and even in the arts. People are constantly jockeying for advancement, awards, accolades, social status, fame, and various positions and opportunities. We want to make more money, own more gadgets, earn more praise, and have more "friends" than everyone else. Have you ever stopped and looked at how many human activities are framed as competitions? When we're born into a culture that suggests that life is a fight for survival from birth, is it any wonder why we're so stressed out all the time? When it comes to our root chakra, we're dealing with the most primal instinct in us: to survive. Therefore, it is important to keep this energy center balanced and harmonized so we don't end up experiencing life as a struggle to survive when we are meant to experience the joy of thriving.

Color
Red.

Location
The root chakra is located at the base of the spine at the tip of the tailbone.

What It Is
Our root chakra is our deepest connection to the physical body, our environment, and the earth. It is connected to the qualities of grounding, structure, ancestry, community, stability, finances, security, and, most fundamentally, survival.

Body Parts
Physically, this chakra is connected to our skeletal structure, teeth, kidneys, blood, and large intestine.

Signs of Balance
When the root chakra is balanced, there is a self-assuredness and a confidence that our basic needs will be met. We feel connected to our physical body and secure in our safety. We have a healthy metabolism as well as physical strength, stamina, and vitality. We also feel safe

in our work life and secure in a financial sense. At the most basic level, we feel like we have the solid foundation we need to build our life upon and the necessary resources to grow mentally, emotionally, and spiritually. We also feel a strong sense of belonging in our families and our respective communities.

Causes for Imbalance

Pain and trauma related to experiences of violence, abuse, threatened survival, poverty, homelessness, food scarcity, financial insecurity, abandonment, and betrayal can lead to imbalances in the root chakra. Disruptions in home life, like a breakup, divorce, marriage, new baby, or family loss, can destabilize this energy center as well. Constant travel, especially to unfamiliar places, and living paycheck to paycheck are other experiences that compromise the integrity of the root chakra.

When Out of Balance

When the root chakra is out of balance, we may feel disconnected from our body and show signs of clumsiness or issues with coordination. Poor circulation and arthritis in the lower extremities, spine or skeletal issues, joint pain, issues with legs, knees, and feet may also manifest themselves. Issues with undereating and overeating could also indicate an imbalance in the root chakra as well since they relate to our metabolism.

Emotional and mental signs of overactivity or excessive energy in the root chakra may manifest as fear and insecurity related to the physical body and material matters. We may isolate ourselves, feel disconnected from others, and act aggressively, manipulatively, or even violently to get what we want to feel secure. Believing that there is not enough, that life is a competition and that this world is dog-eat-dog can give rise to root-chakra imbalances that lead us to act harshly and selfishly. We may become addicted to physical pleasures, which give rise to opulence, greed, and an overindulgence in food.

Emotional and mental signs of underactivity or insufficient energy in the root chakra include feeling worried, anxious, fearful, and uncertain about one's place in the world. We may suffer from low self-esteem, low confidence, depression, and possibly even suicidal thoughts. If our root chakra is out of balance, we may be more likely to receive abuse or to abuse others. We may also find it difficult to get a handle on our financial matters and therefore struggle with money or experience poverty. There is also an element of not feeling welcome or not fitting in with our family, community, and society at large.

Mantras

I am strong. I am safe. I am secure. There is enough.

AWAKENING SOUL FORCE

Generating Positive Energy

Taking proactive physical action can generate positive energy flow in this center. Making connections to family members, ensuring that your home space feels safe and comfortable, managing and tidying up your finances, connecting to Mother Earth, and spending time in nature are all physical activities that bring the energy of safety, security, and stability into your life. Even if the direct experience of safety, security, and stability are not fully within physical reach yet, taking actionable steps toward those goals can generate positive energy and momentum in that direction. When you take tangible actions and combine those efforts with consciously working to clear out any negative beliefs, trauma, or energy blocks, you reclaim your right to feel safe, secure, and grounded in this world through your root chakra.

Root Chakra Reflection

At the end of 2018, I felt wiped out and had a severe energy deficiency in my root chakra. This was due to the fact that I was traveling so much for work and for love, which led to my feeling disconnected from a stable, singular home and community. Over the course of that year, I had been working on a congressional race in Southern California as well as a congressional race in upstate New York. My work with PATH had me traveling up and down the state of California, and my girlfriend was permanently living five hours north of me. This is an example of how the busy nature of life can catch up to us energetically. Working with our chakras should be an ongoing process of energetic maintenance, kind of like brushing our teeth!

Think for a moment about what it means for you to feel secure—at home, at work, in your relationships, in your communities, in the world, and in your own body. What do you need to feel safe? Fixed housing? A steady job? Close family relationships? Do you feel supported by these things in your life right now? If not, what other ways can you invite more stability and security into your life right now? This could be as simple as having a consistent schedule and routine for yourself, making small deposits into your savings account so you can begin to build more of a "safety net," regularly connecting with the people you care most about, or spending more downtime in nature.

At first glance, which of the qualities listed above resonate most with you? Based on the breakdowns above, does your root chakra seem balanced, or are you experiencing an imbalance in this energy center? What action can you take to maintain balance or to rebalance this energy center for yourself?

SACRAL CHAKRA

What was your favorite creative activity as a child? What did you like to do? What brought you joy? Do you remember what you were first taught about your sexuality? Was it explained clearly and celebrated appropriately, or is there shame or trauma around sex from childhood? Welcome to the realm of the sacral chakra.

As children, we aren't afraid to express ourselves, whether it's through cartoon drawings or brightly colored costumes. As we get older, though, many of us begin to censor, suppress, or completely ignore these creative impulses. Creativity and unique self-expression are often mocked, looked down upon, and dismissed as "childish" or "unrealistic" by authority figures in our culture. We'd be hard-pressed not to find an actor, an actress, a writer, a musician, or an artist who hasn't been told to "grow up" by people living more conventional lives. What a tragedy it is that our culture has such a calloused view of creativity—one of the greatest and most natural gifts of being human.

Similarly, in a culture dominated by ancient religious views toward sex and sexuality, there's a good chance a lot of us grew up feeling like there was something "dirty" about sex. Sadly, many of us even experienced trauma around our sexuality growing up. We can buck these cultural oppressions and move into a fuller experience of ourselves, our emotions, our creativity, joy, and sexuality by tuning up our sacral chakra.

Color
Orange.

Location
The sacral chakra is centered between the pelvis and the navel, about two inches below the belly button.

What It Is
Our sacral chakra is connected to the qualities of the emotional self, creativity, sexuality, sensuality, fun, and play.

Body Parts
Physically, this chakra is connected to the health of the reproductive and sex organs, kidneys, bladder, spleen, lower back, hips, and large intestine.

Signs of Balance
The sacral chakra is a beautiful energy center. It is the seat of creativity, relationships, intimacy, sexuality, feelings, and emotional life! When the sacral chakra is

in balance, we experience the joy of life. We're open to experiencing pleasure simply for the sake of pleasure. We take time to indulge in recreation and play. We freely express our creativity, not just through "art" but through artful living. We also freely express our emotions and are capable of a good laugh as well as a good cry. We know and understand that sex is a healthy part of our own personal experience and feel free to express and enjoy our sexuality in a pleasurable and fulfilling manner.

Causes for Imbalance

Issues in the sacral chakra can arise if we grew up in a household with strict or rigid rules and restrictions, particularly around creative, emotional, or sexual self-expression. Parents or authority figures who displayed coldness or apathy toward our feelings can cause a disturbance in this chakra as well. Any experience of having our creativity or emotions rejected, scrutinized, or criticized can cause an imbalance in this energy center. We can also harbor trauma in the sacral chakra if we experienced any kind of sexual or emotional abuse or manipulation.

When Out of Balance

When our sacral chakra is out of balance, it may physically manifest as pure physical exhaustion, chronic low-back pain, or pain in the pelvic and hip regions.

Kidney problems, as well as urinary and bladder problems, may also manifest here. Infertility, menstruation issues, prostate, and uterine problems can be physical indicators of sacral chakra imbalance. Since the sacral chakra is also related to the lower intestines, constipation, and diarrhea can also physically indicate excessive or underactive energy in this center.

Emotional and mental signs of insufficient energy in this chakra include feeling emotionally cold, unenthusiastic, and passionless. Pessimism, feelings of unworthiness, and shameful thoughts can also indicate a blockage in the sacral chakra. We may also experience a low sex drive, feel creatively uninspired, and lack confidence in our ability to express ourselves creatively. If our sacral chakra is underactive, we may have a hard time expressing our emotions, experience moodiness, and feel antisocial or invisible to the world.

Excessive energy in the sacral chakra can manifest itself as being melodramatic, feeling emotionally overwhelmed, or even being emotionally aggressive or passive-aggressive. A hyperactive sex drive, sex addiction, and promiscuity can all be indicators that there is an excess of energy in this chakra. This may also manifest as feeling overly attached to others or addicted to pleasure in an unhealthy manner. Jealousy and possessiveness can often arise in these instances.

Mantras

I embrace joy. I embrace my creativity. I embrace my sensuality. I embrace my sexuality.

Generating Positive Energy

Making time for recreation, pleasure, and joy can infuse this center with positive energy. Taking up a creative hobby, such as writing, dancing, music, art, or crafting, can satisfy the creative aspect of the sacral chakra. Exploring sexuality and sensuality in ways that are healthy and stem from your true desires can also bring healthy energy into the sacral chakra. Generally, relaxing, having fun, and taking responsibility for your emotions can help balance this energy center. When you take tangible actions and combine those efforts with consciously working to clear out any negative beliefs, trauma, or energy blocks, you reclaim your ability to create and experience joy from the seat of your sacral chakra.

Sacral Chakra Reflection

As I mentioned earlier, I tend to have an abundance of sacral-chakra energy. This makes it extra crucial for me to be conscious and aware of how I wield this energy and where I direct it. When I am creating from my soul, whether writing, shooting, editing footage, or taking photographs, my sex drive tends to feel relatively healthy and balanced since so much creative energy goes toward my projects. When I'm creating from my soul, I am also emotionally expressing myself honestly and freely, which keeps the sacral chakra flowing well. If I am not creating from a place of inner truth or if I cease to create at all, my libido will kick into hyperdrive. When my sex drive kicks into an abnormally high gear, I now know this means it is time to reflect on where am I not expressing myself freely. This pattern only came into my awareness thanks to my studying and working with the chakra system over time.

Think for a moment about any deep emotions or creativity that is yearning to be expressed through you. How do you best like to express yourself? Are you a poet, a musician, a builder, or a gardener? What would be the most satisfying creative outlet for you to participate in? What one small action can you take this week toward allowing yourself to indulge in your own creative expression? Perhaps it's buying paint supplies, jotting down ideas for a story, or planting a new flower in your garden.

At first glance, which of the signs and characteristics listed above resonate most with you? Based on the breakdowns above, does your sacral chakra seem balanced, or are you experiencing an imbalance in this energy center? What action can you take to maintain balance or to rebalance this energy center for yourself?

SOLAR PLEXUS CHAKRA

Growing up, did you have the experience of feeling like your own person? Did your parents and authority figures give you the freedom to explore your interests, express yourself, and experience the world in your own way, or were there expectations placed upon you to behave a certain way? In a world where everyone wants you to see the world the same way they do and live up to their version of life, it can be tough to carve out your own path as an individual. There is an immense amount of institutional and social pressure to conform, to follow, and to play by someone else's rules. Sometimes it's easy to forget we were blessed by our Creator with free will and all of the spiritual, emotional, and physical faculties to not just exist but *thrive* in this world in our unique way. The solar plexus chakra is linked to the ways that we carve out our own identity, develop the inner strength to be and express who we are, and create a life based our own truths—not someone else's beliefs or rules.

Color
Yellow.

Location

This solar plexus chakra is located directly below the tip of the sternum and above the stomach.

What It Is

The solar plexus chakra is related to our personal power, identity, ego, and mental intellect. It is connected to the qualities of self-worth, self-esteem, confidence, and personal will.

Body Parts

Physically, this chakra is connected to our muscles, digestive system, liver, and gallbladder.

Signs of Balance

When our solar plexus chakra is balanced, we feel empowered and confident in ourselves and our abilities. We display an aptitude for balance, self-control, and self-discipline. Physically, we take care of our body by exercising and feeding it adequate food and nourishment. Emotionally, we are optimistic, responsible, and reliable while also remaining adaptable. With a balanced solar plexus chakra, we're able to walk the line between being assertive and in control and remaining humble and open to taking new directions.

Causes for Imbalance

Overbearing authority figures can undermine the personal power we're meant to harness in the solar plexus chakra. This includes not only our leaders, who set the social standards and literally write the laws we follow, but also domineering or controlling parents, bosses, friends, romantic partners, or any other relationships that undermine our own inner authority. The influence of dictatorial or authoritarian governments and religious institutions that require submission and blind faith can also suppress our own personal identity, diminish our individual power, and erode solar plexus energy.

When Out of Balance

Physically, when the solar plexus is out of balance, we may experience stomach problems, eating disorders, food allergies or intolerances, and indigestion. Metabolic syndrome, diabetes, adrenal fatigue, and complications in the liver or small intestine are a few of the ways that an imbalance in solar plexus energy may manifest itself. Chronic stress, panic attacks, frequent illness, muscle cramps, and multiple sclerosis can also be physical indicators that we need to revitalize this energy center.

When there is not enough energy flowing through this energy center, we lack the willpower, courage, confidence, and the self-discipline necessary to fully be ourselves in the world. We may experience fear, anxiety, and self-doubt as well as have a tendency to be overly critical of ourselves. We may also have a negative body image or look for other ways that we're "not good enough." Being trapped in a victim mentality or having a sense of insecurity or inferiority are key indicators that we need to bring more energy into the solar plexus chakra. Underactivity in this energy center may also manifest as people-pleasing and allowing others to walk all over or take advantage of us.

When there is too much energy in this chakra, we may overcompensate for those deep-seated feelings of being "not enough." This could include being judgmental and critical of others, looking down on others, acting unethically, or being aggressive and domineering. Too much energy in this center may mean we become obsessive over our appearance, physically arrogant, and vain. Excessive flow of energy in the solar plexus can lead to a misuse and abuse of power, violent outbursts, and authoritarian behavior.

Mantras

I am confident in who I am. I love my body. I am powerful. I am free.

Generating Positive Energy

Taking care of your body with adequate movement

and uplifting activity can help revitalize this energy center. Honoring your wishes, exercising your free will doing the things you love to do, following your gut instincts, and getting into the habit of pursuing the things you really want in the world are vital to empowering yourself from the inside out. You may not be able to tackle all this at once, but if you make a commitment to really honoring who you are in small ways every day, you will build energy in this center. When you take tangible actions and combine those efforts with consciously working to clear out any negative beliefs, trauma, or energy blocks, you reclaim your personal power and take responsibility for bringing this chakra into balance.

Solar Plexus Reflection

After I got divorced, the energy in my solar plexus chakra was completely stagnant. I was emotionally broken and energy-depleted. During our four-year relationship, in which I was often emotionally manipulated and verbally abused, I had begun to experience the physical signs and symptoms of an energy imbalance in my personal power center. My stomach wasn't well, and I was wrestling with what I thought was potentially a gluten intolerance. Also, on two occasions, my doctor had me tested for diabetes because of high blood sugar levels—a problem I'd never had before or since. Rebuilding the strength and stamina of this energy center was vital to my personal recovery once I left this relationship and set out to reclaim my personal power.

Think for a moment about what makes you feel like your brightest, most empowered self. What makes you feel confident and powerful? Which aspects of yourself are you most proud of? Which of your characteristics do you find the most valuable? Perhaps it's your gentle heart, your great sense of humor, your positivity, or your adventurous spirit. Maybe it's your pop-trivia knowledge, your basketball skills, your culinary creations, or your poet's soul. How can you allow these aspects of yourself to come forward and shine more in your daily life?

At first glance, which of the signs and characteristics listed above resonate with you? Based on the breakdowns above, does your solar plexus chakra seem balanced, or are you experiencing an imbalance in this energy center? What action can you take to maintain balance or to rebalance this energy center for yourself?

HEART CHAKRA

While organized religion as an institution has never resonated with me, the teachers and teachings at the center of many of the world's traditions have. The philosophies of Christ and the Buddha have perhaps had the most profound and lasting impact on me and my spiritual trajectory. These masters share a common dedication to living spiritual principles that resonate deeply in my heart and soul. The heart chakra is at the center of soul force. It is the energy center where the highest ideals of the spirit meet the grounded, physical action of the body and can be expressed through demonstrations of peace, compassion, and nonviolence. To serve as inspiration for bringing our heart chakra into alignment, I want to share a few of my favorite heart-centered quotes from a few of my favorite influences:

> *Therefore all things whatsoever ye would that men should do to you, do ye even so to them: for this is the law and the prophets. (Matt. 7:12)*
>
> *Ye have heard that it hath been said, Thou shalt love thy neighbour, and hate thine enemy. But I say*

unto you, Love your enemies, bless them that curse you, do good to them that hate you, and pray for them which despitefully use you, and persecute you; That ye may be the children of your Father which is in heaven: for he maketh his sun to rise on the evil and on the good, and sendeth rain on the just and on the unjust. For if ye love them which love you, what reward have ye? do not even the publicans the same? And if ye salute your brethren only, what do ye more than others? do not even the publicans so? Be ye therefore perfect, even as your Father which is in heaven is perfect. (Matt. 5:43-48)

Overcome the angry by non-anger; overcome the wicked by goodness; overcome the miser by generosity; overcome the liar by truth. (Acharya Buddharakkhita, trans., **The Dhammapada: The Buddha's Path of Wisdom** *[Kandy, Sri Lanka: Buddhist Publication Society, 1996], sec. 223)*

Color

Green (sometimes with pink).

Location

This chakra can be found right in the center of the chest.

AWAKENING SOUL FORCE

What It Is

Our heart chakra is connected to the qualities of peace, love, forgiveness, compassion, unity, purity, and innocence. It is also our healing center and the chakra through which energy flows when we engage in healing arts such as Reiki, chiropractic work, massage therapy, or hands-on healing.

Body Parts

Physically, the heart chakra is connected to the heart, lungs, circulatory system, arms, and hands.

Signs of Balance

When the heart chakra is in balance, we are open to giving love, compassion, and kindness to ourselves and others as well as to receiving love, compassion, and kindness in return. When our heart chakra is open and flowing, we create safe, supportive environments for ourselves and others, free from judgment. Being open, compassionate, nonjudgmental, and supportive begins with ourselves. "Do unto others as we would have done to us" is an effective mantra if we have the full capacity for self-love first. We have to love ourselves first before we can truly love another. When the heart center is thriving, we see and love ourselves honestly and therefore can fully share love with others.

JEFF BOMBERGER

With the support of a balanced heart chakra, we also know when and how to say no, both for our own sake and for the sake of others. We're good about drawing boundaries and teaching people how to love us. We know that this ability to set and respect boundaries goes two ways: we ask people to honor and respect our true nature, and in turn we honor and respect the true nature of others.

It is also important to know that the heart chakra is the mediator between the earthbound lower chakras and the heavenly upper chakras of spirit. In other words, it is through the heart chakra that heaven and Earth converge and our ability to live and breathe life into the loving presence of soul force is made possible. The heart and solar plexus chakras are closely linked as a strong sense of self-worth supports the self-love required to give and receive love openly through the heart center. The heart's relationship to the chakra above it, the throat chakra, which is the energy center related to truth, integrity, and communication, is vital for us to move through the world in a loving manner. When our heart is open and we speak and live our truth in the world, we bring soul force into powerful alignment. An awakened and expanded heart chakra truly is a gateway into the higher states of consciousness we're going to explore in the next three chakra centers.

Causes for Imbalance

Being a victim of physical, mental, and emotional violence and abuse can all lead to disruptions in the heart center. Being subjected to volatile people, relationships, and all forms of authoritarianism can create blockages in our heart chakra. Harsh punishments, bearing unfair burdens, and betrayal of love or friendship can also throw the heart center out of balance. When someone hurts us, we sometimes hold on to anger and resentment for this person and even ourselves. Having difficulty forgiving others and ourselves can throw this chakra out of balance. When we are reeling from the loss of a loved one, we may harbor grief deep in our heart. If this is left unresolved, our deep-seated grief can turn into a blockage of heart energy.

When Out of Balance

When our heart chakra is out of balance, this may physically be expressed as issues related to the heart and circulatory system. We may experience coronary issues, changes in heart rate or blood pressure, blood sugar imbalances, and blood disorders. Complications with our lungs (which help to oxygenate the blood) and respiratory system, such as lung cancer, asthma, and breathing difficulties, can be a manifestation of imbalances in our heart chakra as well. Muscle pain, tension, or spasms can plague the arms and hands as well as the upper back if we have an energy disruption in our heart center.

If the heart chakra is underactive, we may display a lack of compassion toward ourselves or others. We can experience low self-esteem and low self-worth, which can then lead to martyrdom, feeling taken advantage of, and constantly seeking validation as we try to fill up this energy center from outside of us. A heart-chakra imbalance can also manifest itself as many fears: fear of betrayal, fear of intimacy, or fear of rejection, to name a few. An underactive heart chakra may also be expressed as intolerance, resentment, and holding on to grudges. If this energy center is low on power, we not only have a hard time giving love but also receiving it.

When there is too much energy in the heart chakra, it can manifest as being codependent or overly self-sacrificing as well as giving too much of oneself. This could also lead to becoming possessive, obsessive, and clingy in relationships. We also may find ourselves smothering others with love and affection to the point that it is uncomfortable for others in the relationships. If we are overflowing with heart-chakra energy, we might be moody, melodramatic, and even emotionally domineering. Ironically, too much heart energy can lead to being quick to anger, temperamental, and prone to violent emotional outbursts.

AWAKENING SOUL FORCE

Mantras

All love is within my heart. I feel love and compassion for myself. I feel love and compassion for others. I am love.

Generating Positive Energy

Showing gratitude, expressing appreciation, and being generous toward others allows heart energy to flow freely. Fostering social connections with people who share your values, whether they be family, friends, or new connections met in your community, is another good way to open the heart chakra. Self-love is an important aspect of this center; therefore, affirmations of self-love and acts of self-care can be helpful. Being open to receiving compliments, kindness, and gifts from others is a beautiful way to welcome positive energy into this chakra as well, as is sharing hugs and watching heartwarming movies. Spending time connecting to the serene harmony of nature is yet another, more subtle way of bringing the heart energy into balance. When you take tangible actions and combine those efforts with consciously working to clear out any negative beliefs, trauma, or energy blocks, you reclaim the ability to give and receive love with ease, as this energy purely flows through the heart chakra.

JEFF BOMBERGER

Heart Chakra Reflection

Balancing my heart center is a constant work in progress for me. I opened up this discussion with an example of a powerful heart healing I sought and received in my shamanic workshop. In the intro to the chakras section, I also referenced a breath work session where I did some pretty intense heart-center exploring to root out unresolved feelings that had managed to create an energy blockage. As an empath and someone who feels this world deeply and intensely in the heart center, I probably spend more time maintaining and balancing my energy in this chakra than I do in any of the others.

Think for a moment about how you like to give and receive love. How can you show your care and compassion for others? Maybe you could write notes of gratitude to your loved ones. You could show your best friend great affection by giving him or her a big hug the next time you're together. You may even want to dedicate some time to a charitable cause you feel passionately about. Don't forget to look at what makes you feel most loved and cherished as well. You could take yourself on a date once a week, schedule regular time for your meditation practice, or allow for some physical pampering now and then.

At first glance, which of the signs and characteristics listed above resonate with you? Based on the breakdowns above, does your heart chakra seem balanced, or are you experiencing an imbalance in this energy center? What action can you take to maintain balance or to rebalance this energy center for yourself?

THROAT CHAKRA

How many of us have a hard time trusting politicians? Why is it that they so often don't resonate as real and authentic? In my opinion, it is because many times what they say and do can be contradictory. Sometimes the words they say in a single sentence are contradictory in and of themselves. When we feel this from someone, we're feeling the lack of alignment and the energy imbalance present in their throat chakra and the way it interacts with ours. If our throat chakra is out of balance, we may be susceptible to falling for doublespeak because the throat chakra is also connected to listening. If we tune up our throat chakra, we will not only be better at speaking our own truth, but we'll also be able to detect when someone else is being disingenuous. This energy center is all about alignment and integrity.

Color
Blue/turquoise.

Location
The throat chakra is located just above the clavicle, centered on the neck.

What It Is

Our throat chakra is connected to the qualities of communication, inspired creativity, truth, and integrity. It's where we speak both *the* truth and *our* truth and stand up for what we believe in. The throat chakra also allows us to listen deeply and is connected to teaching. Most importantly, the throat chakra is connected to spiritual integrity and telling the truth.

Body Parts

Physically, this energy center is connected to our throat, ears, mouth, upper chest, shoulders, and neck.

Signs of Balance

When the throat chakra is in balance, we are able to communicate our heart and our ideals clearly, peacefully, and honestly. Our thoughts, desires, and feelings are expressed authentically and truthfully. Talking the talk, walking the walk, and walking the talk all speak to the integrity of a well-calibrated throat chakra. A good sense of humor, timing, and charisma can all radiate from balance in this energy center. Alignment in the throat chakra also makes us great listeners, which means that we not only hear what is being said clearly, but we also hear what is not being said by others. We are able to listen with our other senses, including our "sixth sense," or intuition. We're present and open to what others are trying to say, yet we exercise sound judgment and are more discerning about what we hear. This chakra also governs teaching and learning.

Causes for Imbalance

Growing up in a strict household with oppressive or restrictive parents can block throat-chakra energy if we're forced to swallow our words, so to speak. Living under politically oppressive or authoritarian regimes can also dramatically affect our ability to speak our truth. Not being able to express anger, living with abuse, or being subjected to verbally abusive environments are also common reasons we may withhold what we want to say or the truth of who we are, out of fear of a backlash. Embellishing facts or telling lies can also cause an imbalance in the throat chakra as this erodes our integrity.

When Out of Balance

When our throat chakra is out of balance, it can physically manifest as difficulty communicating. This could appear as a speech-related issue such as stuttering, "losing" one's voice, or a raspy or timid voice. Other problems in the throat region, including coughing and laryngitis, could also indicate an issue in this chakra. Pain and issues in the mouth, such as toothaches, mouth ulcers, cold sores, and swollen or bleeding gums, are other physical symptoms that may call us to work with this energy. Complications in the sinuses, like allergies, stuffy nose, and sinus infections, and pain or stiffness in the jaw, neck, and upper shoulders may also require throat-chakra balancing.

When we are lacking sufficient energy in the throat chakra, we experience problems communicating and have difficulty voicing our thoughts, feelings, and opinions. We may have a literal fear of speaking and have a hard time standing up for ourselves. When our throat chakra is underactive, we may not trust our intuition and our inner voice and will therefore have a hard time being honest with ourselves and others. Sometimes an imbalance in this center can lead to our being manipulative and deceptive with our words and not speaking or living our truth. Blocked creativity and self-expression can also be an indicator that we need to bring more energy into the throat chakra.

When we have overactivity in the throat chakra, we may find ourselves talking too much and too fast, leaving little room to listen. Excessive energy in this chakra might manifest as our speaking negatively about others, aggressively asserting our opinions, or being verbally domineering or even abusive. Gossiping, condescension, and interrupting others can be signs we need to ground some of this energy from our throat chakra. Getting on our soapbox and being preachy, dogmatic, and self-righteous are also signs that we need to bring this energy center into balance.

Mantras

I hear the truth. I speak the truth. I live the truth.

Generating Positive Energy

Finding safe, nonjudgmental, and comfortable spaces to speak your truth and use your voice can be a great practice for bringing new, positive energy into your throat chakra. Join a speech-and-debate club. Try Toastmasters. Give stand-up comedy or improv a whirl. Express yourself through writing, music, poetry, or art. Face your fear of speaking up in places where it is safe to do so. Using your physical voice by singing, chanting, or toning can also help bring balance back into the throat chakra; so can listening to music we really enjoy. This center is also connected to teaching, so mentoring someone and sharing knowledge can strengthen our throat chakra.

Our heart chakra and our throat chakra are also very closely linked, so it is important that we are able to live and speak what is in our heart. Spiritual integrity is of the utmost importance to realizing our soul force and living our ideals; therefore, practicing what we preach is vital to bringing energy into balance in this center. When our heart energy is aligned with our throat energy, we move through the world with a greater degree of integrity, which is vital to empowering our soul force.

Throat Chakra Reflection

Being someone who has strong opinions regarding the injustices perpetrated by governments and politicians, I have long worked with my throat chakra to strengthen this energy center and ensure it remains in powerful alignment with my highest truth. Several elections ago, I worked on staff for an incredibly talented candidate who, unfortunately, treated the staff very poorly during my time there. The candidate and I had a relatively solid working relationship because I may very well have been one of the only people who would stand my ground and say no from time to time.

One morning, several weeks out from the primary, our candidate sat the twelve or so paid staff members down around the table and proceeded to go through the room and, one by one, verbally demolish each staffer in front of the entire group. When it came to me, the candidate said, "You and I, we're fine. You're doing great work." The candidate then continued mowing down one exhausted staffer after the next. The tense room eventually fell silent. My stomach physically tightened in knots. I raised a tentative hand. "Can I say something?" I managed to mutter. "I'm really uncomfortable with what just happened." I then proceeded to stand up for the team as a whole and expressed how hard everyone had been working. I didn't think it was fair to publicly shame everyone, and I certainly felt that this behavior was out of alignment with the campaign mission. Many of us had left jobs or taken temporary leaves to join the team, and we were all working for the same goal: a better, more just government.

When I left the meeting, my body felt physically sick. The amount of emotional toxicity in the room was palpable in my being. Many of the staffers came up to me throughout the day and thanked me for speaking up. The truth is that I didn't say anything revelatory. I simply said out loud what the staff was privately languishing over day in and day out. In private, I expressed to some of my colleagues that I felt like I was reaching a breaking point and that I might have to leave if the behavior didn't change. This confession was met with mixed responses ranging from "that takes a lot of courage" to "the candidate is just taking on negative energy from Washington." I was not buying the latter story.

Needless to say, the next morning, I met privately with the candidate and expressed, in more detail, my concerns with the behavior I'd been witnessing and experiencing. When it looked like there was little chance of reconciling the behavior, we decided it was best I leave the campaign. As an empath and someone who is extremely energy sensitive, the toxicity of the campaign was wearing on me, even though it wasn't directly pointing at me. It was such a shame for this particular campaign to have gone this way, because the message was so potent and the vision so inspired. At the end of the day, I was proud of myself because I spoke up and defended others who I felt were being treated unjustly. I owe finding this strength to the power of doing clear and conscious work in my throat chakra.

Think for a moment about when and where you feel most free to express who you really are. Do you live and speak your truth consistently, or do you change who you are around certain people and in certain situations? What would fully living and speaking your truth look like to you? Can you try journaling your true feelings onto the page? Maybe it's time to have that difficult conversation you've been putting off for a long time. Perhaps you could go out of your way to appreciate and validate someone who you feel is being overlooked. In what one small way can you use your voice more fully or honestly this week?

At first glance, which of the signs and characteristics listed above resonate with you? Based on the breakdowns above, does your throat chakra seem balanced, or are you experiencing an imbalance in this energy center? What action can you take to maintain balance or to rebalance this energy center for yourself?

THIRD-EYE CHAKRA

We live in a visual, media-driven information age. Every day, our senses are bombarded with images and visions other people have created with the hopes of influencing our behavior. No one goes into business, Hollywood, or politics to pitch a product that doesn't sell, so these folks need us to see what they want us to see in order to get what they want. That's why there's such big money behind public relations campaigns and marketing efforts. Being able to see deeply and clearly is important not only for our health and energetic balance but also for the world's as well. The content we watch, the products we consume, and the stories we believe become a part of us when we adopt these visions and live them through our actions. Yet what about our vision? What about our ideals? What do we hold true? By awakening our own spiritual vision, we gain the agency to fulfill our duty to ourselves and the world, which is to bring our unique perspective on life, love, freedom, and spirituality into being through our modeled behavior. Learning to tune in to our own psychic abilities, highest spiritual perspective, and enlightened vision is the realm of the third-eye chakra.

Color
Indigo/deep blue.

Location
The third-eye chakra is located in the center of the forehead, just above the brow.

What It Is
The ability to see both our inner and outer world clearly is the domain of the third-eye chakra. It is associated with the qualities of wisdom, intuition, psychic ability, witnessing, discernment, imagination, intuition, justice, and ethics.

Body Parts
Physically, this chakra is connected to our brain, skull, nose, eyes, central nervous system, and pineal gland.

Signs of Balance
When the third eye is in balance, we are able to focus, concentrate, and enjoy a state of mental clarity. We are perceptive and willing to accept the truth, no matter how good, bad, or ugly it looks. Our intuition is sharper, which means that we are more able to read between the lines and use proper discernment. We rely on our direct experience and our inner soul-force

authority to guide our beliefs instead of listening to authority figures. Clear seeing allows us to put ourselves in people's shoes, see from different perspectives, and achieve a higher, more spiritual perspective that transcends black-and-white, dualistic thinking. Spiritual insight, increased psychic ability and awareness, access to higher wisdom, and inspired visions are also benefits of a well-balanced third-eye chakra.

Causes for Imbalance

Rigid thinking and overintellectualization can create an imbalance in the third-eye chakra. Imbalances in the lower chakras can also cause blockages in this energy center. Being overly emotional or judgmental of others, as well as acting arrogantly or egomaniacally, can throw our third eye out of balance. Substance abuse and addiction will also cloud our vision in this energy center. Denying our spiritual self and believing that this world is simply a material machine can cut us off from the flow of psychic and spiritual energy that is meant to pass through the third-eye chakra.

When Out of Balance

When the third-eye chakra is out of balance, it may physically manifest itself as issues related to the nervous system and the brain. Neurological disorders, dizziness, headaches, seizures, and balance issues may be physical indicators that the third-eye chakra needs attention. Blurred vision, blindness, and sinus issues can also arise if there is an imbalance in this energy center. Mental illness, psychological issues, nightmares, and psychic exhaustion are all physical signs we need to balance the third-eye chakra.

When we have too much energy flowing in the third-eye chakra, we may find ourselves living in a total fantasy world and excessively daydreaming to avoid reality. Conversely, we could find ourselves being too logical or dogmatic in our thinking. In some cases, this could lead to our becoming authoritarian or belittling others in order to impose our vision in an unjust manner. Obsessive-compulsive behavior and paranoia are also signs of hyperactivity in the third-eye chakra. Too much energy flowing in this center can lead to overstimulation of the imagination and hypersensitivity to psychic stimuli.

An underactive third-eye chakra may leave us feeling uninspired, unimaginative, and unable to visualize our hopes and dreams. We may lack clarity and focus, since common sense and spiritual insights both seem to escape us when there is insufficient energy in this energy center. Our thinking may become too rigid and linear. We may view life from a very narrow and subjective point of view, unable to see ourselves and our lives from a higher, broader perspective. When we are lacking in energy in this center, we also are cut off from our psychic senses.

Mantras

I see clearly. I see truth. I am open to the wisdom of the divine. I see with the eyes of spirit.

Generating Positive Energy

The third eye is where we get in touch with our mystical selves. It's where imagination, intellect, and intuition meet to give us a holistic view of ourselves and reality. Therefore, using your imagination and engaging in visualization meditations can charge up this energy center. Practicing yoga can also be quite helpful for the third eye as this practice turns our attention toward conscious breathing and inner life. Creating a relaxing and harmonious environment that allows you to go inward can be helpful in accessing the more subtle aspects of yourself and opening up to inner wisdom. Sleep is incredibly important for the health of the third-eye chakra as well.

This chakra is all about seeing deeper—going beyond what is on the surface and getting into the more ethereal, energetic essence of what is. When we consciously work with this energy center to allow in higher wisdom and expanded spiritual vision, we reclaim our personal power and the ability to heal ourselves in a significant way.

Third-Eye Chakra Reflection

In the spring of 2016, I found myself participating

JEFF BOMBERGER

in a week's worth of protests and sit-ins in Washington, DC. I'd made my second trek in three years, in order to protest corruption in Washington. This time around, I found myself participating in a large act of nonviolent civil disobedience on the steps of the Capitol, as seven hundred of us were arrested and thrown in Capitol paddy wagons for sitting in and "unlawfully obstructing a Capitol walkway" on our first day of protests. Oddly, the experience of being put in handcuffs for a peaceful demonstration—which was meant to bring awareness to the grave injustices of denied voting rights and governmental corruption—was inspiring.

The night before I boarded my flight back across the country, I was overwhelmed with inspiration to run for Congress as an independent in my home district. The filing deadline to get on the ballot had long passed, but I could still register as an official write-in candidate and, at the very least, become a part of the conversation. As a grassroots candidate hoping to amplify the discussion, I launched a robust social media campaign, full of slick videos and honest talking points around the issues I most wanted to give voice to: peace, freedom, equality, and, most urgently, clean government. I received a lot of flak from local activists, who claimed I was going to steal votes and ruin the election, which I knew was virtually impossible from the start.

AWAKENING SOUL FORCE

The bottom line is that I was intuitively and unequivocally compelled to run an unconventional campaign, give voice to the issues that were important to me, and use digital video to get my message out quickly and efficiently. I did not win (which I never expected to), but my experiment worked, in that my small campaign garnered quite a bit of attention in a short time frame. Fast-forward two years to my first meeting with a then-unknown candidate with no political experience named Katie Hill. For those of you who don't follow politics, Katie is, at the time of this writing, the second most powerful representative on the House oversight committee—and she's only thirty-one years old.

Neither Katie nor I would have guessed that my short seven-week experiment in the 2016 primary election would provide a significant foundation on which we'd build her very successful grassroots campaign in 2018. Just like I had before, we ran an unconventional campaign from the outset, gave voice to the issues that were most important, and used digital video to get the message out quickly and efficiently. As an unknown candidate, Katie was willing to take a political risk by being unconventionally open, human, and vulnerable in her run for Congress. In the beginning, we had a camera on her all the time, and the goal was to help her really connect with folks on social media who would otherwise not hear about her until she could raise enough money to air TV ads. We felt that this would give her an early edge with potential voters, over the already-established candidates within the political circles. The vision was fine-tuned as we honed this collaboration together and ultimately ended up with her being elected.

The moral of the story is that it's important to follow your intuition and your ideals, even if you don't know what the end result looks like. Your vision may not be understood, and it may even be unpopular. I could have easily not followed my impulse to run my guerrilla campaign, knowing that I would never win, but instead, I ran because I had ideas! I had a vision that played to my highest human ideals and our better nature, and I wanted to test it in real life, even if not everyone understood what I was doing and why. I had zero intention of being involved in the 2018 election cycle until Katie called me, based off of a referral, and wanted to meet with me. Once we got to talking, and she heard my reasoning for doing what I did, she immediately saw the vision and expanded on it. And so was the beginning of Katie's very wild, improbable, and successful rise to becoming the first woman to ever represent our district.

Think for a moment about when your intuition told you something that proved to be true. What was your intuition telling you? How did the information come to you, and how did it feel? What was the outcome of listening or not listening to this instinct? In what small way can you connect more deeply with your own deep inner wisdom this week? Could you make room in your day for five minutes of meditation, go to bed a half hour earlier, or simply set up a peaceful space in your house to sit and be with yourself?

At first glance, which of the signs and characteristics listed above resonate with you? Based on the breakdowns above, does your third-eye chakra seem balanced, or are you experiencing an imbalance in this energy center? What action can you take to maintain balance or to rebalance this energy center for yourself?

CROWN CHAKRA

You and I, we are one with God. We are the divine experiencing itself as human beings. We are human beings experiencing ourselves as the divine. I know we've all heard words like these before, but a few months ago I had a revelation in one of my meditations in which this truth became crystal clear to me. You see, for too long we've accepted this notion that God is our superior and we are his subordinates. We believe that God rules over us, telling us what to do and how to do it. This is a top-down, authoritarian view of God.

Imagine how our lives would transform if we thought of God not as a parent or a spiritual dictator but as a partner and a collaborator. How would your life shift if you saw God as a loving friend? As I meditated on this conception of God, I asked myself, "What's in it for God for us to be having all this experience? Why create this at all?" Then it hit me. As if my mind had been peeled wide open to allow the wisdom of spirit to emerge, I suddenly and very clearly recognized that we are a mirror for God. We are a reflection and a point of view from which God gets to know and experience his divinity as we move closer to ours. In that moment, I felt the most beautiful, expansive sensation vibrating throughout my entire body.

Those who love us unconditionally—our family, our friends, and our partners—hold a mirror up to us and say, "Look, this is who you are in my eyes. This you offer me, and this I offer you." Think about the joy and the gift of sharing that bond, in honoring and discovering that connection for all the wonder it brings. In this same exact way, we exist in relationship with our divine Creator. No one else on this planet and *nothing else in this universe* is going to have our personal perspective, our unique blend of experiences, or our interests, insights, and wisdom. In that way, the only thing God truly wants from you and me is to see himself, know herself and experience God incarnate as you and me.

Consider that the next time you sit in your meditation. Reflect on that the next time you look up into the eternal night sky. Take a moment and pause. Allow yourself to sink into the knowing that right in that moment, what you see, what you feel, and what you experience are directly linked to God. Your peace in that moment is God's peace. In the moments when you feel joy and wonder or when you feel heartache and sadness, know that God feels that too. Know that your revelation and your spiritual growth unlock a new dimension of relationship with God. In remembering that this is, in fact, an equal relationship, you can then open yourself up to what God wishes to share and offer you in return. After you've sent God your feelings of hope or despair, know that, in an instant, God will respond back and bless you with the love and grace that is eternally yours to share. This is the gift of the crown chakra.

Color
Violet.

Location
The crown chakra is located at the top of our head.

What It Is
The crown chakra is our direct link to the divine source of creation. This chakra is one of my personal favorites because it represents the essence of this entire journey—the remembrance that we all have a direct link to our divine source of creation and the reconnection to our own living, breathing soul force. Experiencing unity and realizing that every single thing in this universe is connected is the gift of our crown chakra.

Body Parts
Physically, the crown chakra is related to our central nervous system, brain, brain stem, cerebral cortex, and spinal cord.

JEFF BOMBERGER

Signs of Balance

When the crown chakra is in balance, we feel a deep sense of interconnectedness and spirituality. We feel connected to our higher selves and to the universe as a whole. We recognize and live in the awareness that we are spiritual beings having this human experience. We view our spiritual path and the path of others not as retribution or punishment for sins but as opportunities to learn, to grow, and to know ourselves as the divine source from which we come. We enjoy the privilege of learning how to transform our spiritual truth and ideals into thoughts, words, and deeds that align with our highest philosophies. We also learn to surrender to this part of ourselves that holds higher perspective and live with the courage to make choices that serve our soul's highest purpose, even if those choices don't always play to conventional wisdom. In that way, we are unshakeable in our faith and walk in alignment with our own highest spiritual, visionary qualities.

Causes for Imbalance

Crown-chakra blockages can be created by self-limiting beliefs peddled by religious authorities. Fear of eternal damnation, going to hell, or being punished by God erodes our relationship with the divine and can lead to blockages of the crown chakra. Indulging in acts of spiritual ego, such as persecuting someone for their spiritual beliefs or feeling resentful because someone has an "easier" spiritual path than us, can also create a blockage in this energy center. If we find ourselves jealous of another person's perceived spiritual progress or gifts, we are engaging in acts of spiritual ego and diminishing our own unique, divine gifts, which throws our crown chakra out of balance.

When Out of Balance

When the crown chakra is out of balance, we may physically experience issues with our nervous or immune systems. Epilepsy, Parkinson's disease, and multiple sclerosis may be connected to an energy imbalance in the crown chakra. We may have skeletal and muscular issues as well as experience a lack of coordination or exhaustion. Autoimmune disorders, cancer, and life threatening illnesses can all be manifestations of an energy imbalance impacting the crown chakra.

If we have an overactive crown chakra, we may end up addicted to spirituality and neglect the needs of the physical body. We may be severely disconnected from earthly matters and become impractical or fanatical about our spirituality. This can also lead to spiritual arrogance, authoritarianism, and feeling spiritually superior to others. Overactivity in this center can also make us gullible and susceptible to spiritual brainwashing.

If we are lacking energy in this center, we may feel abandoned by God, disconnected from our higher self, and lacking in purpose. With that comes confusion, hopelessness, and spiritual depression as a result of feeling disconnected from soul force or our spiritual life force. We can also suffer from being overly cynical around spiritual matters or, on the flip side, being chained to dogmatic or limiting religious beliefs. When this chakra is underactive, we may feel misunderstood, lose our conscience, and perhaps even feel suicidal.

Mantras

I honor the divine and the divine in me. I am one with God. I am one with the universe.

Generating Positive Energy

Meditating on our connection to the divine, to love, to our most expansive soul force is extremely important to balancing the crown chakra. This is the energy portal through which we connect to the universal soul, and it is the gateway to establishing and honoring a relationship with higher dimensions of love and wisdom. There are practices and exercises we are going to discuss in later chapters that will give you some tools for connecting to this aspect of self. Quiet time, stillness, and meditation are essential to creating a thriving connection to the divine through our crown chakra. Practicing yoga is also an excellent way to open and balance this chakra. Showing compassion toward others, walking in faith, and connecting with your spiritual community or tribe are also great ways to bring positive energy flow into this energy center.

Crown Chakra Reflection

For this reflection, I don't want to make any suggestions or share any particular experiences from my point of view. I simply want you to reflect for a moment about your spirituality and your relationship with your divine Creator. What is your conception of God and the divine? What does spirituality mean to you? How do you conceive of a higher power? What dimensions of higher wisdom does your divine entity embody, and how do you most purely connect with this?

At first glance, which of the signs and characteristics listed above resonate with you? Based on the breakdowns above, does your crown chakra seem balanced, or are you experiencing an imbalance in this energy center? What action can you take to maintain balance or to rebalance this energy center for yourself?

CHAKRA-BALANCING MEDITATION

In this chapter, we're going to go through a meditation exercise that aligns and balances the chakras. Think of this practice as an energetic reset button. You don't have to do this whole routine every time you balance your chakras. I'd recommend checking in with your seven wheels of energy every week to see how they're doing and perform maintenance as needed. Since there are seven chakras and seven days of the week, you could choose to have a simple routine of focusing on one chakra a day, spending some time working with and meditating on the energy presently being carried within that energy center. You could also set aside time once a week to do all of the chakras at once or maybe create some other schedule that makes sense to you.

Remember, this journey is about your finding a practice that is helpful for enhancing your life and helping you realize the best version of yourself. For the purpose of building strong energetic foundations, we're going do one pass at all the chakras, from the root to the crown, to get you started. We'll be working with mantras, as well as visualization, to help bring the chakras into balance, and we'll also be using our grounding cord to get rid of any excess energy that needs to be shed in order to attain balance. After we've gone through this whole thing once, feel free to adapt the practice to what feels right for you!

When you do this practice, remember to always start with a soul-force-field meditation to ease you into relaxation; from there, you'll be able to intuitively navigate the energy in each of the seven chakras, beginning with the root and balancing them from the bottom up. So take a moment now to get into a meditative state, using the soul-force-field meditation. Once you've thanked Mother Earth for her abundance and you've invited in divine light, love, and protection, turn your attention to your root chakra by focusing on the area at the base of your spine. Take a few deep breaths and see how the energy in this part of your body feels. What does it feel like? Is there movement? Is it vibrating? Swirling? Pulsing? Sit with any thoughts, feelings, or physical sensations that arise. Allow revelations to emerge. It is not uncommon to feel tingling, warmth, or other sensations that indicate energy is moving around in an energy center when we bring quiet attention to it. Any emotions and thoughts that surface when we begin to explore a chakra can indicate experiences, feelings, and beliefs that need further exploration. Go with how the energy flows, and remember, you can always return to your breathing if your mind feels like it is wandering.

Next, I want you to imagine what this energy center looks like. How does it appear to you? Is it vibrant and expansive? Is it bright, or is it cloudy? How does it feel? This is where you must trust your intuition and go with whatever arises for you. If you tap into the root chakra and you see nothing—no light, no spinning wheel of energy, no color—then there's a good chance you'll want to power up this energy center. To do so, imagine yourself being surrounded by a bright and energetically charged red light. Breathe this red light in, and silently repeat this mantra "There is enough." You could also choose any of the other mantras that I listed in the chakra section—whichever resonates most with you. As you breathe deeply, feel the energy of your root chakra swirl in a clockwise direction. Stay here, breathing in and out, until you feel like this chakra is "full" or properly charged.

If, on the other hand, it feels like there is an overabundance of energy in your root chakra, you're going to want to use your grounding cord, which you set up in the soul-force-field meditation, to help release any unnecessary energy from this center. You can do this by simply breathing deeply and imagining the excess energy as red light being sucked down the grounding cord and into the earth. Repeat this breathing and visualization until the chakra shrinks to a size that feels appropriate and manageable for you. Trust your instincts and intuition on this, and let it guide you through the process. Trusting yourself to balance your own energy is crucial to reclaiming authority over soul force.

Once you finish in the root chakra, move your attention up your body to just a few inches below your navel. Turn your awareness to your sacral chakra, and focus on how this area feels. If this energy center appears to be underactive, imagine yourself surrounded by a bright, magnificent orange light. Breathe in and out deeply, and begin repeating the mantra "I create joy" (or whichever mantra fits for you). As you allow this orange light to move into the sacral chakra, feel the energy of your chakra swirl in a clockwise direction. Stay focused on this point of attention until you intuitively feel like this chakra is full and vibrant. If you're experiencing an excess of energy in the sacral chakra, follow the same grounding-cord guidelines for releasing energy as we used above, this time envisioning orange-colored light being grounded into the earth.

When you're ready, bring your attention to a few inches above your navel, right below the base of the sternum. Focus on your solar plexus chakra and get a sense for how this area feels. If this center feels energy deficient, try charging it up. Imagine yourself being surrounded by bright yellow sunlight while you visualize yourself being who you want to be. What does that look like? What does that feel like? How would you appear in the world? Hold this vision in your mind while repeating the mantra "I have the power to choose." You can always choose another mantra that resonates for you. As you breathe this yellow light in, feel the energy of your solar plexus chakra swirl and expand in a clockwise direction. Continue to focus on increasing the energy in this area until it feels full and this chakra is appropriately aligned. If the energy center is overactive, try the same practice of visualizing yourself embodying the vision of yourself you'd like to be while releasing that excess yellow energy into the ground.

Once you're finished there, turn your focus to the center of your chest; this is your heart chakra. Pay close attention to how this area feels, noticing any sensations, thoughts, feelings, or revelations that arise. If this energy center feels underactive or weak, imagine yourself being surrounded by a bright, vibrant green light. Breathe this light in and out deeply, allowing it to fill up your heart center with peace, compassion, and love. Visualize this energy swirling in a clockwise motion. As you feel your heart energy expand, repeat to yourself, "All love is in my heart," or use whichever mantra feels most true for you. As you soak in the truth and vibration of these words, feel the energy of your heart chakra rise and swirl until you intuitively feel your heart is perfectly full.

If this center is overactive, use deep breathing and the grounding-cord visualization to release any excess green energy from the heart center until you feel it come into a comfortable balance.

When your heart is full, move your attention to the base of your throat, where we're going to work with the throat chakra. Pay attention to any sensations that may come up for you here. If the energy here feels weak or sluggish, imagine yourself being surrounded by a cool, soothing bluish-turquoise light. Breathe this light in deeply and fully; allow this light to enter and revitalize your throat chakra. As the energy increases, imagine the light and energy beginning to swirl in a clockwise motion. Repeat the mantra "I am open, honest, and clear in my communication." Perhaps even speak this mantra, or whatever mantra feels right for you, out loud. If there is excessive energy in the throat chakra, turn your attention to your grounding cord and release that turquoise energy into the earth until you feel the throat chakra is healthy and balanced.

Now move your focus to the center of your forehead, just above the brow, in order to balance the third-eye chakra. Don't be surprised if this center is more visually stimulating than the others. See if any visions, images, or memories pop into your mind. Tune into the frequency of the third eye to see how it appears to you and how it feels. Allow insight to emerge, and if it feels like it needs a charge, begin to imagine yourself being surrounded by a deep, soulful indigo-colored light. Breathe in and out, letting this bright light be absorbed and integrated into your third-eye chakra. As the energy fills, imagine it swirling in a clockwise motion, and repeat whichever mantra your intuition feels is right for you, such as "I am connected with the wisdom of the universe." If you sense there is an overabundance of energy here, breathe deeply and ground that excess indigo energy into the earth until the third-eye chakra feels balanced and aligned.

Finally, turn your attention to the top of your head—the crown chakra—where the beam of white light already merged with you in the beginning of your meditation. Connect to this divine light, and allow it to inspire you. As you bring your attention here, pay attention to any initial thoughts, feeling or sensations that arise. If this energy center needs charging, imagine yourself surrounded by the most comforting, warm, and loving violet light. Breathe in and out, integrating this energy into your crown chakra and feeling it swirl in a clockwise motion. Repeat the mantra "I honor the divine and the divine in me," or choose whichever mantra fits for you in the moment. If you feel there's too much energy flowing in this center, ground some of that violet light into the earth and slowly ease it into balance until it feels fully aligned.

As you wind down, do one more quick pass through

each energy center, then imagine them all swirling in balance together. Give thanks for the opportunity to connect to your divine nature. Announce your intention to move out of the meditation and return to waking life. In your mind's eye, imagine the protective bubble of divine white light encircling you again, and let it be known you are closing the session and wish to be open only to energy that serves your highest good in each chakra. Give thanks for the healing and balance that you will now carry with you into the world. Whenever you're ready, open your eyes.

You have now experienced a full-body chakra meditation. As I mentioned before, you could do this full meditation a couple of times a week, or you could do one chakra a day, depending on your schedule and what feels best for you. Remember, spirit works effortlessly in its own divine timing, so this isn't about more is better. Doing this meditation every day doesn't mean that you're going to achieve enlightenment faster; that's spiritual ego talking. This activity is about alignment, balance, and healing the constantly ebbing and flowing soul-force energy within and around us. You should intuitively move in and out of this work as you see fit. With that said, it's really easy to fall behind on this work as a preventative and maintenance practice, so I would recommend establishing a consistent routine at first; this will allow you to familiarize yourself with the process that works best for you as well as to build a habit. Once you get into a rhythm with the practice, you may begin to notice subtle energy patterns moving and shifting within you throughout the week or even over the month. For me, personally, I do a brief check in every day just to see how everything is doing, then tend to end up focusing on one chakra that feels the most "in need" at that time.

Before we move on, I'd like you to reflect on any thoughts, feelings, or physical sensations you may have experienced as you tuned into each chakra. This will help you to become more aware of the subtle ways that your body, mind, and spirit speak to you. Since beginning this practice, I have definitely become more in tune with my body and the sensations that arise when I'm working in different chakra centers. If I develop a scratchy throat, for instance, I'll look to the throat chakra to see if there is anything blocked or out of balance there. If my chest feels heavy, I know that my heart chakra needs some attention. Don't panic if these kinds of subtle sensations arise in your meditation; it doesn't necessarily mean that you are ailing from a life-threatening disease or disorder. They can simply be indicators that there is some work to be done in a particular area of our body, energy, or psyche.

When thoughts, sensations, or feelings arise during chakra work, it's important that we open up an honest inquiry so that we can identify what's at the root of energetic blockages and disturbances and address them before they grow into bigger issues. As I mentioned before, each energy center relates to different aspects of our spiritual, emotional, and physical bodies. It's our job to get to the truth of why something is arising in our meditation. Essentially, we have to get comfortable asking, "What is this? Why this? Who or what is this related to?" over and over again until we gain the insight and clarity we're looking for. By doing this, we open up a dialogue between our conscious mind and our more subtle, intuitive self. To be aware of unconscious disturbances can alone be healing. I am highly encouraging of being proactive and finding our own answers in order to bring the chakras into balance. Using intuition, imagination, visualization, and guidance from higher wisdom, we can reconcile deep pains and heavy emotions as well as engage in acts of forgiveness toward ourselves and others in order to balance and heal any energies that are out of alignment.

Remember, there is no expectation for you to do this healing work completely alone. Working with trauma or blockages can be challenging, and sometimes we need the outside perspective of someone to help walk us through and facilitate our journey. This is perfectly acceptable, and different people will require different rafts to get to the other side of the healing river. Follow your intuition, and allow your instincts to guide you in your healing process.

BEING ENERGY SENSITIVE

You feel the world deeply. You walk to the beat of your own drum. You're a hope-inspired dreamer, but you've also suffered from bouts of depression. Your friends, relatives, or even random strangers open up to you about their feelings without even asking. After this happens, you might feel completely drained. You like people but need time to be alone to recharge after any extensive interaction with "humans." You probably feel energized by deep personal connections, film, music, art, singing, dancing, and all things expressive. There's also a good chance you once were or still are incredibly creative and imaginative. The latest trends in social media and the news probably leave you feeling angry and depressed after any extended exposure, and, at the end of the day, you wish people understood you better.

If a lot of these statements describe you, there's a good chance you're living the life of an energy-sensitive empath. An empath is a person who is naturally tuned in to the emotions, feelings, and energy of others, including animals and even the vibration of physical locations. Empaths are hypersensitive people and are truly the energetic sponges of the world, which is why this energy work we're beginning to do is so vitally important. In recent years, the acknowledgment that some people experience the world in this way has become more mainstream, which is a great social leap forward. While it is extraordinary that society is beginning to recognize this state of hypersensitive existence, I've realized that for me, it has required quite a bit of diligent soul searching to feel comfortable being an empath in this world.

I say this as someone who has always felt the world in a profoundly deep way. Even after growing up under the guidance of loving and supportive parents who were open to unorthodox ideas, nontraditional philosophies, alternative healing modalities, and psychic phenomena, I still found myself, at the age of twenty-five, not clearly understanding what all these feelings, emotions, impulses, and sensitivities were. I was restless and incredibly hyperactive. Paradoxically, I would also at times feel emotionally wiped out and drained by the social issues plaguing society. I often felt like I was stuck between two worlds, mashed up and spread out in an energetic smorgasbord for anyone's taking. I felt this way until I embarked on a rigorous journey of self-analysis and self-discovery with soul force.

If you're resonating with what you're reading so far, know that you're not alone in the things you feel. In my experience, feeling the world deeply and in a hypersensitive way isn't as uncommon as we often believe. There are simply fewer people willing to truly open up and talk about it. I certainly found this to be true in my decade-long endeavor as a personal trainer in the health and wellness field. It was remarkable to me how many closet "spiritualists" and "feelers" were out there. Usually the subject wouldn't come up until I brought it up, and I was sometimes surprised by the characters who would lean into the conversation and open up about their own psychic experiences. There may well be fewer people who commit to doing the deep inner cleansing required to reject society's conditioning and reclaim their personal spiritual superpower, but hopefully we are already changing that!

Find comfort in knowing that you, me, and anyone else who senses the world in this incredibly sensitive way is not at all strange. Our senses are simply taking in a great deal of information, and we happen to be acutely aware of a wide spectrum of subtle vibrations. As human beings who are energetic and have a high degree of emotional and physical self-awareness, it is our job to make use of these sensitivities to live our best lives and improve the lives of others. These are useful tools bestowed upon us to help us enjoy and cocreate life in ways that are constantly evolving and expansive. I realize that this world, especially in American culture, is not particularly kind to sensitive people. Those who experience the world with more sensitivity can tend to feel like they're taking a psychological and emotional beating for simply existing. Many of us who felt the world intensely and deeply when we were younger were likely told to "suck it up" or to ignore these sensations. As the philosopher Krishnamurti helped guide me to understand, "it is no measure of health to be well adjusted to a profoundly sick society." In my view, it is up to the feelers of the world to be the healers of world.

As empaths, we are caught in this space between feeling deeply and being told not to feel at all. This causes tension, confusion, and inner friction. Those who have been desensitized by choice or by conditioning simply won't share the experience of life's emotional and energetic sensations in the way that an empath might. In turn, because empaths are energetic sponges, we tend to take on the heavy and dense emotional energy that is impressed on us by those who are more rigid and coercive and less aware of their own deep sensitivities. We are also energetically inclined to pick up the dense vibrations that our brothers and sisters find themselves entangled in. This, in turn, can pull us out of alignment with who we really are at our core. Suddenly, the vibration of others begins meddling with our own vibration because we are indiscriminate, open energy channels taking on their energy by sheer proximity. Luckily, there are ways to see and feel through all this in a healthy manner, and that's what we're going to dive into soon.

Even though I was a "popular" football player in high school, I felt very alien and was never quite comfortable in my high school scene. While I loved the game of football, I struggled to feel at home in a culture that reeked of toxic masculinity and ultra-high-stakes prep competition. I loved to play, and I did love to compete, especially with myself. Yet there was always an awareness that I was experiencing the intensity of sports culture differently than most of my teammates or even my coaches. I do feel fortunate enough to have had a strong nuclear family that was and has always been my "tribe." I credit my family ties and relationships as the reason why I never experimented with drugs and alcohol in high school and found my way into meditation and soul seeking instead.

It wasn't until I got older that I recognized that my mom and I share very similar empathic qualities. It has been a gift to recognize this about ourselves, as we both have been able to spiritually grow in very relatable ways over the years—especially now, as adults. I can't stress enough how important it has been for me to feel like I have people out there who "get" me. I feel extremely fortunate that my mom and dad happen to be two of those people for me, because they provided a foundation of love and support and a sense of belonging that is irreplaceable. If you haven't found that tribe yet, rest at ease knowing that there's a whole lot of us out there and that we're finding each other now, more frequently than ever!

I hold the belief that it's crucial for all people, especially those of us who are energy sensitive, to find our way out of being emotionally and energetically crushed under the weight of society's more calloused and insensitive conventions. We have to reclaim our own emotional, energetic, and spiritual vibration through deep work so that we can realize and manifest the gifts we have to offer the world in our own way. Through my own seeking, I've discovered that a great deal of the cultural conditioning we're exposed to flows energy in direct opposition to a state of balance and wellness. To recalibrate ourselves, we must engage in a deliberate, disciplined, and discerning effort to become in tune with our true inner nature. We must work patiently and compassionately with ourselves to heal any and all traumas that have been heaped upon us so that we can, ultimately, align with the soul force within.

We have to work persistently to connect with our authentic vibration and to build our own personal soul force so that we may live full, empowered, creative, and hope-inspired lives. When we live our lives guided by the sensitive, gentle, compassionate nature inside of us, we move into fulfilling and satisfying a deep inner yearning for balance and wholeness. I used to believe

AWAKENING SOUL FORCE

I was a total martian and that there were few others out there like me, until there came a moment when I sensed that this story I was telling myself was a divisive "us versus them" narrative: the sensitive versus the insensitive. Understanding that this life and the universe seek balance, I had to shift my perspective to an "us with them" mentality and recognize we're all working to release the burden of life's sufferings so we can know true freedom together some day.

Five years ago, my sister had the first of her three children. As an uncle, watching my niece and nephews grow has convinced me that we all come into this world as tiny little empaths bristling with soul force. If you want to get a quick download of what our true nature is, look no further than a toddler or a young child. Vibrant. Creative. Curious. Perceptive. Intuitive. Honest. Watching the three of them navigate the world, I realized that all the innate tools we need to thrive are at our disposal as soon as we begin to develop awareness. Children have wonder in their eyes, creativity in their spirit, and movement, joy, and laughter in their bones. They are unbound by convention. They are sincere in their presence. They are completely transparent and brutally honest. This is our natural state! Yet this natural state can be slowly and subtly corroded by a culture that, for some odd reason, seems hell-bent on chipping away at as much of that innate joy, individuality, creativity, and love as possible. To sever the stranglehold society has on our divine nature is our spiritual lift in this lifetime! This is the massive shift we must make if we want to strengthen our soul force.

All this is to say that, fundamentally, we're highly creative, intuitively sensitive, and uniquely quirky beings when we come into this world. The degree to which these qualities remain is determined by our childhood environment and how resilient we are in our effort to heal and reconnect to this true nature. The way our childhood self is nurtured or not nurtured plays a tremendous role in our personal, emotional, energetic, and spiritual development. We really can't hold it against anyone or anything that has lost touch with this innocence—including ourselves—because often this disconnect happens at such an unconscious level.

If I'm being honest, when I look at the big picture, the grand plot in this high-stakes drama we know as life, it seems that this fall from grace is almost necessary for us to truly awaken and fully recognize the soul force within. For anyone who has studied story, myth, or the work of Joseph Campbell, we may recognize this as the universal hero's journey. What begins as a spark of light falls into darkness only to remerge as an even brighter light. What begins as unrealized and improbable potential blossoms into a powerful force that uplifts the hero and humanity around them. We are all on our own hero's journey!

At the outset of this quest, we must first forgive ourselves and others who have contributed to our loss of innocence. We must forgive those who contributed to the blunting of this true sensitive nature because they know not what they have done. We must also forgive ourselves for those moments when we've lost sight of who we really are. We were and are only doing our best with the tools at our disposal in a very particular moment. We must release this guilt and instead turn our focus toward growth, healing, and evolution. With our eyes lifted, we begin to clearly see the path. We heed the call to a brighter version of ourselves, and we accept the task of undoing what the world has done to us. Through this process of self-purification, we aim to be a master of self. We intend to lovingly take control of our lives and once again return to the pure, creative, and conscious spiritual state from which we came. And with that, now it's time to add some more tools to our spiritual toolbox so that we may begin to rediscover and recognize the true power of soul force within.

SOUL-FORCE REFLECTIONS

Cultivating an ability to see ourselves objectively and with loving eyes is going to be vital to discovering and strengthening soul force. If we can learn to see ourselves clearly, to confront and manage both the comfortable and uncomfortable parts of ourselves, we can build our spiritual foundation on truth, self-love, and integrity. When we can see ourselves clearly, we will see the world clearly. When we can be honest with ourselves, we will be honest with the world. When we can forgive ourselves, we will forgive the world. When we love ourselves, we will love the world. When we transform ourselves, we will transform the world.

Engaging in inner study, meditation, witnessing, critical self-analysis, creative expression, and reflection can expedite our personal growth and strengthen our connection to soul force. When we engage in these practices, we take control of our lives and become the stewards of our proverbial ship. When we engage in these practices, we reclaim the power to define who we

JEFF BOMBERGER

are in this world as creators, as visionaries, and as sovereign, free-thinking people. Liberation awaits us on the other side of darkness, pain, trauma and discomfort. Liberation awaits in the light of who we really are. Now it is time to get to work. Now it is time to pull back the veils of conditioning and reconnect to pure soul force within.

DECONDITIONING THOUGHT EXPERIMENT

The story we tell ourselves about humanity and who we are as individuals is going to be at the center of all the reflective work we're going to engage in moving forward. Therefore, before we dive into the next set of practices, I want us to take a moment and engage in a simple analysis of some of our own sponsoring thoughts. A sponsoring thought is a fundamental idea or belief that precedes the creation of all other thoughts. It is the philosophical soil from which the seed of our life springs and grows, which will determine how vibrant our life may potentially grow to be.

Take, for example, the idea that human beings are born sinful and tainted by evil. This is a sponsoring thought about ourselves and all of humanity. If this idea or belief takes root in us, through parental, religious, and social conditioning, before we become conscious and self-reflective, what do you suppose will be the unconscious self-image we develop? Will we view our lives, our bodies, our impulses, and our desires as fundamentally good or fundamentally bad? How do you think the guilt and shame around our humanness that arises from this founding idea may impact the energy flowing in our chakra system?

This is just one example I want to use to illustrate a larger point about what we'll be up to with this thought experiment. Our deepest spiritual and philosophical beliefs, at their very essence, carry an energetic vibration. This energetic vibration can move us more into alignment with our highest conceptions of the divine, love, compassion, and freedom, or this frequency can create an energetic obstacle standing between us and our highest human potentials.

We're going to go through a series of questions and acknowledge the sponsoring thoughts we are currently working with. We are then going to question where our conception came from and whether we have any lived experience that tells us this belief is objectively true. Then we are going to explore whether or not there is the possibility for an alternate sponsoring thought to exist.

At the most fundamental level, do you believe human beings are essentially good, essentially evil, both, or a total blank slate?

> *Why do you believe this? What was the moment when you felt certain of this judgment?*

AWAKENING SOUL FORCE

What has been your personal lived experience? Not someone else's stories, not history books, not what you've seen on the news. In your day-to-day existence, what has been your experience interacting with and relating to other human beings?

Have you ever seen a good person do bad things?

Have you ever seen a bad person do good things?

Is there a possibility you have more to learn and experience before making a broad judgment about all of humanity as a whole?

Are you open to shedding your sponsoring thought for the sake of understanding the whole of humanity more deeply, without judgment?

If you're open to forming a new sponsoring thought about humanity, take a moment to consider what your own ideal vision of humanity is. What new sponsoring thought would support this vision?

At the most fundamental level, do you believe that you, as a person, are essentially good, essentially evil, both, or a total blank slate?

Why do you believe this? What was the moment when you felt certain of this judgment?

What does your lived experience say about you? Put

~ 239 ~

aside what your parents, teachers, friends, bullies, pastors, priests, and television advertisements have told you about who you are or what you've done. In your heart of hearts, when you lay your head down to go to sleep, what does your lived experience say about your moral nature?

Have you ever done things you believed were bad?

Why?

Have you ever done things you believed were good?

Why?

Is there a possibility you have more to learn and experience about your own moral nature before making a broad judgment about who you are?

Are you open to shedding your sponsoring thought about who you are for the sake of understanding yourself more deeply, without judgment?

If you're open to forming a new belief about your moral nature, take a moment to reflect on your own highest vision of who you are. What new sponsoring thought would reflect who you truly are?

At the most fundamental level, do you believe in higher levels of human consciousness, the soul, or spirit?

Why do you believe this?

AWAKENING SOUL FORCE

What does your lived experience tell you about higher levels of human consciousness, the soul, or spirit?

Have you ever felt inspired by higher dimensions of consciousness, the soul, or spirit?

Have you ever felt betrayed by higher dimensions of consciousness, the soul, or spirit?

Is there a possibility you have more to learn and experience about higher dimensions of human consciousness, the soul, and spirit before making a broad judgment about what these conceptions might ultimately be?

Are you open to shedding your sponsoring thought about higher levels of human consciousness, the soul, and spirit for the sake of understanding these conceptions more deeply, without judgment?

If you're open to forming a new sponsoring thought about higher dimensions of consciousness, the soul, and spirit, take a moment to consider what your ideal, supportive vision of those realms would be. What new sponsoring thought would more accurately capture this vision?

Sit with these questions and really take the time to reflect on them. Write down your answers, then take an honest look at how they've shaped your spiritual perspective up until this point. What do these answers say about who you've been? Most importantly, do your answers reflect a point of view that supports who you wish to be moving into the future?

Know that there are no right or wrong answers. We simply want to begin stretching our minds and exercising free thought in all directions around some of the most intimate and profound questions we are faced with as people living in this world. Once you've brought these answers, ideas, and concepts into the forefront of your awareness, let us continue on our reflective journey with more practices.

MINDFUL MEDITATION

One of the important aspects of reconnecting with soul force is disconnecting from all the distractions surrounding us: the scripted droning of news anchors, the buzzing of phones, the flashing of social media notifications, the wants and needs of our partner or family members. Don't get me wrong; all of these aspects of our lives have their significant time and place, and many of the relationships closest to us are sources of great joy in our lives. Yet so much of our time and attention are focused on things outside of ourselves that we tend to lose touch with our inner life and inner voice. When our gaze is perpetually fixed on our outer world, it becomes easy to forget the vast inner universe animating us from within. It becomes easy to forget who we are. Then all of life's problems get infinitely more complex because we lack connection to our own highest vision. The goal of this meditation practice is to spend a little more time getting to know our inner selves so that we have a clear vision, regardless of what goes on outside of us.

For most of my adult life, I've been self-employed. Much of my mind chatter used to come from anxiety around where my next client would come from: Was I doing a good job? Would I have all the funds I needed to pay my bills? Was this really what I was meant to be doing? Should I have been doing something else? Was I stupid for always choosing to be freelance? These were mostly valid questions to ask, and I clearly identified some issues I was wrestling with internally. Yet without creating the time and space to quiet the noise, how could I possibly gain clarity on my situation and let my intuition guide me to my highest good? I had to find a way into a silent space where answers to these questions could authentically arise from a more subtle, loving soul force within.

When I finally did get quiet, I was met with a calm reassurance that everything would be OK. My attention would often be turned away from my worries and drawn to my long history of having my basic needs met somehow, in some way. These silent moments with my soul gently reassured me that living heart centered was the path through this challenging transition I was in. As my spiritual practice deepened, I also became inspired to be more generous and charitable, even when money was tight month in and month out. I remember one eye-opening occasion when I encountered a young man around my age experiencing homelessness. As I walked by him, he said, "Sir, can you spare some change? I'm really hungry."

My first thought was, "Man, I've barely got enough money to stock the shelves in my house." Yet I saw the pain and desperation in his eyes. His plea was sincere. He looked . . . tired. Just a moment of fully taking him in with all my senses, and I knew that this man needed the ten bucks a meal would cost much more than I did. So I asked him his name and told him he could order whatever he wanted from a nearby McDonald's. His eyes lit up when I engaged with him. When I found out that he hadn't eaten in two days, I had not a doubt I was doing the right thing, even if it meant being a little squeezed for cash that week. That same week, I had three people randomly buy me food. I met up with an old friend who told me he wanted to pay for my lunch. I went on a spontaneous date with a woman I had met in my apartment complex, and she insisted on buying dinner. I met a creative colleague for tea, and he rejected my repeated offers to split the bill. This experience taught me the value of honoring the inspiration that comes in quiet moments. It also taught me how to let my heart—not my anxious thoughts—guide my actions and allow the world to work magic in return.

Creating the time and space to let our inner voice authentically arise is exactly what we are aiming for with this exercise. For the next few weeks, commit to a minimum of five minutes of silence. Find a space in your home or go to a peaceful place in nature where you can be alone and in as much silence as you can manage. If total silence is traumatic for you, you could choose to do this exercise with relaxing music or a soothing ambient sound playing softly in the background—or this exercise may not be for you, and there's nothing wrong with that.

On your journey to self-awareness, observing your thoughts and feelings, removed from any immediate stimuli, will be enlightening. When you get in the habit of doing this, you will begin to see patterns in the thoughts and feelings that are scrambling around your mind on a regular basis. If your inner world is consumed by thoughts, feelings, and sensations that have nothing to do with the silence of here and now, this tells you a lot about where your healing work must begin. It shows you the things you must learn to let go of so you can find a path to being more present in the moment.

To begin the exercise, simply close your eyes and focus on your rhythmic breathing. Take a deep inhale to the count of six, hold for a count of three, release to the count of six, and hold for a count of three. Do this a few times to center yourself, feeling your entire body breathe, from the tip of your head down to your toes.

After you perform your initial rhythmic breathing, settle in and see where your mind begins to wander. What you'll likely notice is that there will exist a certain degree of "noise" within your mind. This is normal. It is OK! Don't try to turn it off. Whatever is going on inside the mind is finally coming to your conscious awareness. This is why I prefer to do this exercise in solitude, free of any and all sensory distractions. It is incredibly revelatory to be left alone with our thoughts.

When you sit in this way, what thoughts arise? What do these thoughts say about your focus? What do they say about where you put most of your energy and attention? What insecurities arise? These moments of silence won't necessarily be all doom and gloom; this space should give you a moment to let lighter thoughts arise as well. What hopes, dreams, and wishes come alive in this silence? What do you imagine? What do you dream of? What do you most wish to create? What is your highest vision for yourself? Why? How do you feel in relation to these ideas? Are they comforting? Do they inspire fear or excitement? Do you get butterflies? Are these ideas anxious or liberating? Are they expansive or contractive?

These are some questions you can ask in this resting state, and there are plenty more questions you can pursue the answers to. The key in this exercise is to simply cultivate an awareness of that which populates and permeates your inner life on a regular basis. This window into your internal world will give you an awareness that allows you to begin to more clearly see and feel anxiety, stress, and the voice of the inner ego that has you disconnected from your subtle, authentic self. With this awareness, you can then deconstruct the anxious experience and challenge its existence.

This is a good step in reconnecting with ourselves. In

silence, relatively removed from the activity of the world around us, we shine a light on the chatter that rages on in our inner world. Understanding this realm of ourselves, questioning it, challenging it, and most importantly feeling and acknowledging it, is going to lead to discoveries about our true nature, about what simply is. This requires observation and total honesty with ourselves. No need to ask why you are constantly thinking about someone or something; simply acknowledge it is so and let it go. Look for patterns and repetition. These inner rhythms will be useful as you let go of what no longer serves you and move into living in alignment with your deepest soul force.

Soul-Force-Reflection Exercise

- Set aside a minimum of five minutes a day for yourself to get quiet.

- Increase the duration as your comfort and resolve build.

- Make sure there are no distractions. This time is all about you and being with yourself.

- Longer sessions will yield more discovery as the conscious mind is allowed to let go and wander deeper into the more subtle activities of mind.

- Allow space for dreams and aspirations to arise; these are often important indicators of our highest thought.

WRITTEN-THOUGHT OBSERVATION

For me, personally, I've grown to love sitting in silence. I've come to enjoy the soothing sensation of inactivity or the ambient sounds of my immediate environment. I have even grown fond of the ebbing and flowing of thoughts in and out of my mind. If mindful meditation doesn't resonate with you, another option is channeling your thoughts into the written word. Not only is this technique valuable for exercising mental energy, but it can also be an excellent remedy when we're having difficulty sleeping at night and need to exhaust any rampant thoughts.

 I was only sixteen years old when a journaling assignment in English class changed my life forever and allowed me to discover my authentic voice for the very first time. For several weeks, we were told to keep an ongoing journal. Sometimes we were asked to write about an in-class prompt, and sometimes we were directed to engage in simple stream-of-consciousness freewriting. By the end of the assignment, I had compiled a stack of angsty teenage meditations on life, society, human suffering, and a new political reality that emerged for me after 9/11. There were personal reflections for me as well, but I found what most troubled my sixteen-year-old mind were massive existential, philosophical, social, and political issues. Who am I? What does it mean to be an individual? Who are we as a culture? Why are we here? Why do we treat each other badly? Why is there violence? Why is there suffering? Are we capable of higher love? Is there a path to world peace? What is the reason for this experience? How do we dream bigger dreams? How do we make them real?

I can pinpoint this journaling assignment in Ms. Lawson's eleventh-grade English class as the precise moment where I launched an even deeper inquiry into the nature of myself and the world around me. This journaling assignment helped me discover a subtle but resounding voice within that was perpetually searching for answers. When I removed myself from the hustle and bustle of football practice, classwork, and teenage heartbreak, there was a part of me, deep down inside, that not only felt the world deeply but also wanted to understand it more intimately. The practice of journaling allowed me discover the issues my soul was yearning to be at peace with—from having to share homeroom with the cheerleader who broke my heart to the havoc American foreign policy was wreaking on the international community. This was an incredibly healthy way to keep my emotions flowing. For the first time, I saw my innermost self begin to take shape in the form of words on a page. As this became a deeper practice for me, I eventually found myself getting in touch with my feelings and a true, authentic voice I came to know as my higher self.

As a teenager, I had a lot of mental energy. I still do. Taking up writing helped me wrest control over my own anxious thoughts and philosophical musings alike. Journaling is still my number one go-to when I am feeling overwhelmed and unclear about what is going on in my world. When I have racing thoughts at bedtime that meditation cannot quell, I often turn to journaling to ease my mind. If you have high anxiety or mental energy, written-thought observation might be a helpful tool to gain some perspective on yourself. For me, being able to see my thoughts outside my head always gives me a clearer looking glass through which I can process and assess my internal world. It puts my thoughts out in front of me, where I can dissociate from them and reflect on them more objectively than if they remained inside my mind.

There's a saying: "Thoughts become things." A lot of times, the things we experience in our day-to-day lives truly begin as simple, unconscious, or rogue internal thoughts. Due to our propensity for what is referred to in Zen as "monkey mind," we can often become exhausted by our relentless mental activity. If our thoughts are random, anxious, and chaotic, should we be surprised if our experience of the outside world feels just as random, anxiety inducing, and chaotic? Because thoughts become things, our experience is profoundly shaped by these very erratic thoughts within the mind.

In this way, the chaos inside our minds gives rise to a chaotic experience of the world we perceive to be outside of us. Anxious thoughts lead to anxious experiences because our experience of the outside world is an extension of us. When we believe all the world is an injustice, we see nothing but injustice in the world. When all we have is a hammer, everything looks like a nail. By getting our inner thoughts out on paper, we can look at them in a way that allows us to see ourselves more clearly. When we see what's going on inside more clearly, we can then see what's going on "outside" more clearly as well. Finally, by doing this, we realize there is no inside and outside world; it's all one, and we're cocreating it all of the time at the level of perception.

If we're looking to experience more peace, more balance, and more harmony, then we must create that space within. If we want to uncover the power of our own personal and unique soul force, then we must set our intentions on aligning our thoughts, words, and deeds with this subtle yet powerful aspect of self. This can be done through the following practice.

Like with mindful meditation, begin with committing to five to ten minutes of what I refer to as mind dumping. Set a timer, then let go—just write. Don't think about what you're writing about. Don't meditate beforehand. Just dump. Unload whatever is on your mind onto the page. It doesn't matter what you write, only that you keep writing, without stopping, until the timer goes off. You may even find yourself writing beyond the timer because you've opened the floodgates.

The reason I call this exercise "written-thought observation" is because writing down your thoughts manifests their quality in a concrete form you can read, observe, and analyze. You can physically see them with your own two eyes. Your words, the phrasing you use, and even your handwriting will transfer energy from your inner life out onto the page. The words and language you choose will have weight and provide insight into your emotional state. Short, profanity-laden sentences reflect a very different state of mind than long, flowing sentences with flowery language. Pay attention! The handwriting itself will be an excellent barometer for your internal energetic condition. Frenetic letters, chicken scratches, cursive, or well-rounded and precise print can all signal various states of mind as well. Sometimes I can visibly see my hurt and my anger transform into hope and aspiration through the handwriting itself. It's as if the act of writing alone is physically working out the emotional and energetic kinks I'm experiencing internally. What starts out as very rushed and sometimes illegible scribbling can transform into more clear, deliberate pen strokes after a few lines or paragraphs. This is of great value to the observer and one who seeks to be in tune with oneself and because it is handwritten, it reflects a degree of truth that pounding away on a phone or computer keys cannot reveal.

    Remember, these activities are about self-awareness. How can you change, recreate, or transform your relationship to soul force if you have no idea where you're starting from? The key in this activity is to write freely, without judging yourself. This becomes an act of self-love all on its own. If what you write is dark, fantastical, perverse, dreamy, or idealistic, simply get it out of you and acknowledge it. Look at it. It's important for you to see your mind chatter for what it is. It's important to exercise your inner voice. This practice is as much about getting to a point of clarity beyond the chatter as it is about serving as a valuable form of self-expression. Bottling up energy and emotions is a great form of constriction that leads to frustration, friction, and unease within ourselves. Taking on a journaling practice can help unblock uncomfortable thoughts, feelings, energy, and emotions. Bringing these inner matters to light is a big step in becoming more self-aware. The more in tune you are with your present state of being, the more you create the space for conscious transformation.

AWAKENING SOUL FORCE

Soul-Force-Reflection Exercise

- Write daily, at the same scheduled time if you can or whenever you feel your emotions becoming uncontrollably aroused. First thing in the morning, midday, or the end of day are great times to mind-dump and expel any anxious thoughts or feelings.

- Give yourself solitude so you can get in touch with your inner voice and work in a space free from fear or judgment. Alleviating fear clears space for your authentic self to emerge.

- If it helps, set a timer for five, ten, or fifteen minutes and just begin writing, without thinking about what comes next. Write until your timer goes off, or, if you're so inclined, keep on writing until the thoughts and feelings exhaust themselves. You may be surprised by how much lighter you'll feel if you give yourself permission to fully express yourself without limits.

WITNESSING MEDITATION

A few years ago, a really beautiful illustration for this witnessing meditation came to me in one of my own mindfulness sessions. In my mind's eye, I saw a conveyor belt, which slowly cycled along in front of me. At first, there was nothing on it; yet as I continued to watch the traveling belt, a very nondescript box suddenly came into view. I focused my attention on this box, watching as it continued past me on the conveyor belt, until it drifted out of my line of inner sight. I then focused my attention back on the blank space directly in front of me where the conveyor belt continued to move along at its steady pace. What came riding into view next was an image of myself looking extremely angry. My first thought was "That's interesting." Yet almost as quickly as I could be in full awareness of this impression, the image was already moving along the conveyor belt and out of my inner sight.

Next came a portrait of someone from my past who I did not want to see, and I had an immediate emotional response. In my mind's eye, I reached out, grabbed the photograph, and began to question what she was doing here in my meditation and why. Years of anger, sadness, and heartbreak began to flow as I held this photograph in my imaginary hands. After a moment of indulging in these intensely triggered emotions, a big yellow ball of light came drifting along the conveyor belt. I was so consumed by this photograph that by the time I noticed the yellow ball of light in my peripheral vision, it was gone. I realized that while I was busy dwelling on the image in the photograph and getting twisted up in the emotion it triggered, I had missed the opportunity to be fully present with a really lovely sensation of light that had come and gone just as fast as the rest of the images. This shifted my awareness and my attention profoundly. I put the photo back on the conveyor belt, and it too finally drifted away and out of sight. This meditative vision taught me the fundamentally transient nature of thoughts, emotions, sensations, and, essentially, life. I realized that holding on to emotions—both good and bad—means missing out on being present with what is right here and now.

When we can remain immersed in loving, nonjudgmental awareness, we are in flow with soul force. We allow life to flow along, and we flow with it, knowing that both the pleasant and the unpleasant shall pass. In previous chapters, there have been ample opportunities to turn our conscious awareness inside and out so we may know ourselves and the world of our inner impressions more deeply. We've attempted to bridge the gap between

AWAKENING SOUL FORCE

our environment and how we feel. We've taken a critical and analytical eye to the potential truths our chakras reveal. We've also taken steps, with both mindful meditation and written-thought observation, to become more aware of our inner life and to engage with it, transform it, and express it so that a more subtle, pure, and powerful force within may arise. Now we are going to practice becoming a witness of the mind by simply observing our thoughts and emotions as they arise, without trying to change or understand them. At its essence, this witnessing meditation is the practice of creating distance between the observer and the observed, which allows us to let go of the thoughts, emotions, and sensations that arise for us as soon as they are ready to pass, thus letting the conveyor belt move things along naturally.

You will want to perform the soul-force-field meditation and rhythmic breathing to ease you into a state of relaxation before doing this exercise. This will also allow you to set the intention that you are holding steady in the light of your soul force and that you will only retain energetic impressions that serve your highest good. After you settle into a safe and sacred space, you are going to simply sit and watch thoughts, feelings, and sensations as they come and go for five to ten minutes. This is different than in the mindfulness meditation, when we looked at what was coming up, noted patterns, recognized the content of our thoughts, and reflected on what they may say about where our energy and attention often are. In this exercise, do the opposite and turn off that analyzing mind. The goal is to detach yourself from thoughts, feelings, and sensations that arise to the point that you watch them in a nonjudgmental manner, without engaging in the emotion attached to these sensations, just as if you're watching projections on a movie screen.

As you become more familiar with this practice, you'll begin to cultivate a new perspective—one that is not immersed in your inner sensations but is in *relationship* to them. By creating space between who you are and what you think and feel, you may remain in the pure truth of your ever-present soul force while allowing the transient nature of thoughts, feelings, and emotions to come and go naturally with ease. You'll gain a clearer picture by allowing sensations to simply exist as passing experiences rather than identifying with them. For example, rather than identifying with sadness or being consumed by betrayal, you can honor yourself as pure soul force having a transitory experience of sadness or betrayal. Instead of identifying with joy, you can remain grounded in your soul force, allowing the sensation of happiness to come and go. Whatever the sensation, you can let it go from your experience because "this too shall pass."

Thoughts, feelings, and emotions are important on

AWAKENING SOUL FORCE

our journey and in our lives; they are vital signs of the quality and integrity of energy being exchanged. Emotions may not always accurately reflect reality as it is, but they are important perception signals for us to honor, look at more deeply, and calibrate. I do not believe eradicating ourselves of thoughts, feelings and emotions should be the objective of meditation practices because these are aspects of self and tools for us to use in navigating our relationship with life at a level of conscious awareness. After all, we must know when our food is spoiled so we can avoid sickness. We must know when a person is emotionally toxic for us so we may draw proper boundaries. We must be aware when our body is tired so we may give it rest. We must honor pain in our joints as it may indicate injury. Our humanness isn't a burden; it's a vital aspect of who we are in this lived experience.

Our thoughts, feelings, and sensations allow for an inner dialogue to take place within the system that is our mind, body, and soul connection, but we mustn't mistake them for our true nature. By allowing ourselves to acknowledge our thoughts, feelings, and sensations, we both honor them in the moment and give them the freedom to be organically released from our experience moment to moment. This practice can keep our soul-force vibration high as we identify less and less with our fluctuating and fluid emotional life and remain more in alignment with the well of unconditional love and compassion existing within. As we strengthen this perspective, we can more easily ebb and flow with the currents of life, both free to be aware of life's sensations and free to let them go. This is living with soul-force awareness.

Witnessing-Meditation Exercise

- Set aside a minimum of five to ten minutes a day for yourself to get quiet, observe, and witness your inner life.

- Perform the soul-force-field meditation at the beginning of the exercise to orient yourself from your highest perspective.

- Refrain from judging and engaging with your thoughts, feelings, and sensations. Simply acknowledge them and let them go.

- When you finish with your meditation, see how long you can remain in this perspective with your eyes open. Develop a practice of allowing an experience in, acknowledging it, and letting it go.

CREATIVE SELF-EXPRESSION

I looked at the red numbers glowing at the back of the room. There were still forty-seven seconds left in the longest two minutes of my life. There was an uncomfortably long silence as I paced back and forth on the tiny cracker-box stage. Around thirty stone-faced comedians stared up at me from under the glare of the house lights.

"Who here goes to the gym?"

Not a single soul humored me.

"*No one here's ever gone to the gym?*" I playfully shot back to the silence.

Somehow the stagnant room got even more deafeningly quiet. Thirty-six seconds on the clock. I looked back at the uninviting faces, and I broke. My mic hand started to shake.

"All right, thank you so much!" I said as I waved to the lifeless crowd. I threw the mic back into the mic stand as fast as I could and darted offstage right for the nearest exit.

For a moment, I stood outside of the tiny comedy club in Santa Monica, feeling totally humiliated that I had bombed a simple two-minute routine. "That was

JEFF BOMBERGER

awful," I thought to myself. I leaned back against the brick building and forced myself to take some deep breaths. As I did, I could hear the comic after me going through his set. He was faring just about as well as I had. It suddenly hit me that even though no one had laughed while I was up there, no one had been laughing before I got on the stage either. Now there was a new comic, and still no one was laughing. In that moment, I realized that maybe I wasn't failing at anything. More importantly, I recognized that the audience's reaction shouldn't matter anyway because I didn't come to the open mic for them. I came for me!

At that particular point in my life, I had decided to try a couple of open mic nights in an effort to get comfortable being really uncomfortable speaking in front of a crowd of people. Even though I had just run for Congress and given physical voice to my own very personal truths, I still felt like I needed to become more comfortable being more vulnerable, and by that measure the evening had been a success. I identified the feelings washing over me as shame and disappointment that had been left over from my days as a child actor whenever I would fail to book a job or get a certain reaction from the audience. This early conditioning (by no fault of anyone's) had created a sense in me that I had to constantly strive to be "good enough" and to please an audience.

When I recentered myself in my intention for being

there at that open mic night, in an instant the years of people-pleasing and the shame and humiliation that had been triggered simply washed away from me. While this experience did not exorcise these feelings from my being altogether, it helped me make a massive leap to a new level of understanding and comfort in my own personal development. Despite years of social conditioning telling me that I was supposed to be entertaining up there on stage—that I needed to make them laugh and they needed to like me—I grounded myself in remembering I showed up to say my piece, regardless how it was received. Within moments, I went from feeling embarrassed to feeling empowered. By honoring and acknowledging that there was value in showing up to express myself simply for the sake of expressing myself, I felt a rush of confidence. This experience is the precise purpose of this chapter.

    If you're like me and where I've been on my journey, you might engage in certain activities and take certain actions for a desired result or outcome. Can you think of a time when you've taken action specifically for a simple reaction? Can you think of a time when you've taken action not for the sake of the action itself but as a means to a worldly end? We go to work to make money. We write papers to pass class. We learn a trade so we may be able to turn it into a business. We clean the house so our significant other will appreciate how wonderful we are.

JEFF BOMBERGER

This list could go on forever. One of the life lessons I've come to value deeply is the art of doing something simply for the sake of doing it. In this practice, we discover the inherent value of presence and *being* while doing happens. This means that we are going to practice taking away the desired emotional or physical goodie from the outcome of our actions. Instead, we will practice immersing ourselves in the process of being present in our experience so that we can enjoy and appreciate the experience itself.

Ultimately, this means we're going to set an intention to engage in work for the sake of losing ourselves in the work. Have you ever seen a Tibetan Buddhist sand mandala? Tibetan monks will spend days, weeks, and even months carefully crafting this beautiful and intricate sand mandala only to destroy the piece once it is finished. The lesson of the sand mandala, of living in the moment and the impermanence of all things, is the lesson we seek to gain wisdom from in this exercise. This means writing that paper for the sake of expressing oneself fully in that particular moment. This means learning a trade for the sake of the process of discovery that it provides. This means cleaning the house for the sake of being consumed by the simple act of cleaning.

While all these other examples are tasks we could mindfully explore alone, for the sake of our purposes here and connecting with our soul force, I want to focus

AWAKENING SOUL FORCE

on engaging in creative self-expression because learning to enjoy the process of creation and self-expression has become one of the most joyful lessons life has taught me thus far.

Have you ever fully recognized how wonderfully creative children are? Observe your own children if you have them. If you have a grandchild, niece, nephew, or neighbor, you can witness them in their own element too. If you're not around kids much at all, go back into memories of what you spent your time doing in your childhood. Isn't it inspiring to recall the amount of time and energy kids spend simply playing and creating? When music plays, babies bounce in their bouncy chairs. Kids dance almost instinctively at the playing of any tune. Give a toddler some markers, and they color all over everything—both inside and outside the lines! Join a child in their world of make-believe, and you can fill an afternoon with imaginary heroes and adventures. Remember, this was our true nature before we were told to "grow up." Remember, this was our true nature before someone told us our drawings weren't good enough. Remember, this was our true nature before we were told our singing voice was annoying. Remember, this was our true nature before we were asked to reject our wild imagination for an adult's less magical version of reality.

The innate impulse to self-express is undeniable,

yet our culture collectively suppresses this in almost every way possible. Our priests, our parents, our teachers, and even our artistic coaches begin to impress their version of the world onto us: *this* is how it *should* be. They subtly and sometimes not so subtly require us to express ourselves in ways that are in alignment with their vision and their values, based on what they've come to know and learn in their experience. This is not all bad; sometimes these visions and values lead us to better versions of ourselves and our own deeper truths. Sometimes this wisdom puts us on the fast track to spiritual growth. Other times, these visions and values divorce us from our better nature and the innermost truth we were meant to bring into existence through our own being. Sometimes another person's experience can become our wisdom. Other times, another person's knowledge becomes our prison. We have to be willing to give ourselves permission to express what is inside of us and explore these mediums in our own unique way. We must allow ourselves to create freely, purely, and without judgment if we want to touch the gift of soul force within us.

I am not going to ask you to take up piano to become the next Beethoven. Wanting and desiring a particular outcome defeats the purpose of what you can explore here. Take up the piano because it makes your soul sing, because you feel like Beethoven when you play "Mary

AWAKENING SOUL FORCE

Had a Little Lamb." I am not asking you to pick up a video camera and become the next Stanley Kubrick. Pick up that camera and find your own unique perspective in the world, and then you will discover you really are your own Stanley Kubrick. Take singing lessons so you may come to know and love the sound of your very own distinct voice. Join an improv troupe or community theatre so you can revel in the joy of losing yourself in an imaginary world of pretend. Create art that you are free to share or not share with anyone because this art is for and about you, not anyone else.

You may very well discover a unique talent and aptitude for artistic expression. Other people may love what you're painting, writing, singing, playing, or creating. You may even find a new vocation by engaging in this exercise! Or you may not. Any and all of that is OK, and frankly all that matters on this soul-force journey is that you're purely expressing yourself. When I was twenty-five, I decided I would make a return to acting as a change from the health and fitness industry. Since I had done the actor thing as a kid, I figured I could easily step back into the game and maybe make some money doing it. However, what grew out of my return to acting class led to so much more than gigs and paychecks. It reignited a creative spark and passion in me that had been dormant for a long time. With that came a creative curiosity that would rapidly transform my life within a

JEFF BOMBERGER

matter of a few years.

I view returning back to acting classes as a pivotal choice that led to opening the floodgates of my own creativity. I learned a lot about myself when I got back into class. I was suddenly forced to become more aware of my own energy and emotions. I was also asked to be able to control that energy and emotion, to a certain degree, in an effort to effectively play other human characters. Being the spiritual seeker I am, I immediately began drawing parallels between acting and life. I soon found acting class wasn't enough to satiate my creative hunger, and neither was the occasional gig. So I began writing scenes and monologues I could perform on my own or with friends. This cracked open a whole new creative process: the act of writing and crafting scripted scenes.

I would then workshop these scenes with other actors, but this also wasn't enough, so I picked up a camera. With that camera, I began filming myself and my friends performing the scenes we'd written. Of course, I had dreams and visions of working on big Hollywood projects, but at some point I became so enamored with the creative process itself that I got into the flow of creating just to create. I was having so much fun learning about cameras and editing software and meeting new and interesting people that I kept creating out of the sheer joy of creating. Eventually, I let go of the conceptions I had about where I thought I should end up and just let

AWAKENING SOUL FORCE

the creative force flow where it wanted to flow without any desired outcome, and, as fate would have it, I found a second career producing digital content. I want you to find this flow for yourself, regardless of whether anyone ever sees your art or not, because this artistic practice is about awareness, discovery, and expression!

The moral of the story here is that creative self-expression is an exciting and invigorating process. It is a reflective journey all on its own, and it is invaluable what we can and will learn about ourselves and this world if we venture to observe, to reflect, to mirror, and to create. The more we open up to it, the more we realize there is a magical quality to unleashing and honoring this aspect of ourselves, because creativity is very much part of our nature. I can't help but share the sentiments of the novelist Kurt Vonnegut: "Practicing an art, no matter how well or badly, is a way to make your soul grow, for heaven's sake. Sing in the shower. Dance to the radio. Tell stories. Write a poem to a friend, even a lousy poem. Do it as well as you possibly can. You will get an enormous reward. You will have created something."

For the sake of knowing yourself and honoring your inner voice, I want to encourage you to take up some sort of creative hobby—whatever you're interested in. It can be something you used to do as a child. It can be an art form you've always wanted to explore. It can be something you're really great at or a craft you're maybe

JEFF BOMBERGER

not so good at. Talent, or a lack thereof, by whoever's standards, is completely irrelevant. Your action is all about the intention: learning the art of expressing yourself and creating for the simple sake of expressing yourself and creating. Many of my own life lessons, insights, and realizations came from willingly throwing myself into the abyss of being a beginner in many art forms and just enjoying the ride. When I was twenty-five, I didn't know how to use a camera. I didn't understand film lighting. I didn't understand script and story structure. I didn't know my way around a Mac computer, its pro-grade editing software, and I certainly didn't know what the heck coverage or dailies meant.

Eight years later, I know a whole lot about that stuff I once didn't know, and that alone is fun. Eight years later, I haven't sold a Hollywood script, but I still love to write scripts. Eight years later, I haven't directed or edited a feature film, but I still love making digital content, commercials, and little movies whenever I can and when I'm called to. Eight years later, I'm not being paid to be an actor, but I still love improv and role-playing if I get the chance. Through creative self-expression, I've learned valuable lessons about authenticity, vulnerability, and, most importantly, who and what I am spiritually—a creator. I've learned what it means to be resilient and persistent. I've learned to let go. I've learned there no such thing as failure; there's just try,

AWAKENING SOUL FORCE

evaluate, try again, reevaluate, and try again, over and over. The satisfaction of having crafted, built, or created something from start to finish is second to nothing in my experience. I've learned what it means to love yourself and what you create for exactly what it is, nothing more and nothing less. I've learned a great deal about myself, about people, and about life through creativity. I feel I would be cheating you out of one of life's most wondrous experiences if I didn't recommend creative self-expression as a path to recognizing and realizing your own inner soul force.

So come on now! What will you create? What's the book you've been dying to write? Which local theater is holding public auditions for *Romeo and Juliet*? What's the next fashion trend you'd love to see make a comeback? What words of wisdom and beauty are yearning to spill forth from your heart and onto the page? What handy project has been calling you to the garden for months or even years? What do your hands want to build? I know there is an artist in you. I know because we are all artists and this life is our canvas. Give yourself the space and the permission to create. No one has to know. No one has to approve or praise you. No one has to pay you. I want you to create. I want you to create for you. I want you to create because creating is what you were born to do. Creation is essential to the living, breathing, thriving soul force within you.

Circle all of the creative outlets that interest you:

Acting	Hairstyling
Architecture	Improv
Art	Interior design
Baking	Karaoke
Building	Knitting
Choir	Landscaping
Coloring	Makeup
Computer programming	Music
Cooking	Painting
Crafting	Photography
Creative writing	Poetry
Crocheting	Puzzling
Dancing	Quilting
Daydreaming	Sculpting
DIY projects	Singing
Doodling	Sketching
Drawing	Spoken word
Engineering	Sports
Exercising	Video games
Fashion	Writing
Gardening	Zumba

Self-Expression Exercise

- Once a week, set some time aside to create something new.

AWAKENING SOUL FORCE

- Draw a picture, paint a painting, join an improv troupe, take an acting class, dance to your favorite music, sing karaoke, play dress-up, write a poem, pick up an instrument, build a piece of furniture, cook a new recipe—anything your creative heart desires!

- Create in a safe, nonjudgmental space. By that I mean don't judge your own work, don't show it to others (unless you want to for sharing purposes), and don't compare your work to anyone or anything else!

- Embrace being a beginner and enjoy the process of creating and discovering.

- Be mindful and aware of what you are inclined to create. What kind of stories do you want to tell? What do you like to draw? What kind of photographs do you prefer shooting? I believe our art often mirrors our inner state. Again, don't judge this. See it for what it is. Acknowledge it. Love it. Most importantly, express it.

- Remember, there is no failure. There is try, evaluate, try again, reevaluate, and try again, over and over. The process is infinite!

SOUL-FORCE CONNECTION

In the same way that muscles need a combination of exercise and nutrition to grow stronger, growing the power of our own inner light, wisdom, love, and creativity requires ample time and attention. In my own practice, I've come to call it "going to the well," as in going to a well of water that fills me up with life, rejuvenates me, and nourishes my vitality. The practice of reaching down into the soul force within allows me to remain in touch with the pure, loving, nonjudgmental, and transformative intelligence residing within me as well as revitalizes me in a way that nothing in the outside world can. In fact, it is this practice of going inward that enhances my relationship with the world I engage with, cocreate, and experience every single day.

"If I don't go within, I go without." This is one of my favorite mantras, and it sums up how vital intentionally connecting with pure soul force has become for me in my daily life. Every day, I take the time to ignite my own inner light so that I may move through my day in a more conscious state of higher wisdom, expanded perception, and heightened human potential. Don't get me wrong: I have my days. It's not all rainbows and unicorns all the time, as healing requires wading through darkness. Emotions can get the best of me, but practice and cultivated awareness have made it easier to pull myself back to center when I am out of alignment. I have come to be so grateful for the life, the love, the insight, the healing, and the wisdom this practice bestows upon me — so much so that I go to the well every single day at least twice a day, even if it's only for five minutes at a time.

In the closing chapters here, we are going to discuss some methods to build a relationship with your soul force within. Now is the time to reclaim your own unique and rightful connection to divine source. Now is the time to reclaim your particular role on this planet and in this universe. Now is the time to communicate with soul force.

CONNECTING TO SOUL FORCE

A direct line to soul force—the vibration of pure love and creation that is existence itself—is our most wondrous gift. It's important to let go of any thoughts and beliefs that would divorce you from this personal divine connection because they do not serve you or humanity's best interest. Fundamentally, nothing in the physical universe can stand between us and our Creator because soul force is everything. Soul force is all, including those who would deny us of our shared divinity. Soul force and I are intrinsically entangled in this universal collaboration. Soul force and you are intrinsically entangled in this universal collaboration. You and I are intrinsically entangled in this universal collaboration through soul force.

This spiritual connection between us and soul force can never be severed. Our relationship to the divine can exist at a distance or it can be ignored, but it never ceases. In that way, it is the truth that persists. Our relationship to the divine can exist intimately and be present in all ways, all the time. Just because we don't always feel a breeze move across our skin doesn't mean the air isn't right there filling up our lungs. Regardless of how aware we are of the presence of the divine, the truth of oneness persists. We are entitled to this relationship with higher wisdom, and it is meant to be cultivated, enjoyed, and experienced by each and every one of us in our very own way. Soul force is omnipresent. Her love unconditional, his wisdom unlimited. We may have access to this vibration if we seek it. Like all relationships, this connection is a two-way street. Soul force is always ready to meet us halfway. It is up to every individual to reach out and make the effort to commune with our creative life force. All we need to make the connection is the time, the space, and the intention to do so.

By reclaiming spiritual authority over our soul force and turning our awareness toward the subtle energies swirling within and around us, we may begin our own interaction with the divine. Opening to this exchange of energy will lay the foundation for a thriving relationship that will lead us to our greatest potential, our most authentic experience, and our personal divine revelation. You may access the wisdom and guidance of soul force, master teachers, and other helping and healing spirits by opening yourself up to love, wisdom, and guidance. Know, though, that you must be sincere in your efforts. Your motivations must also be true. You must sincerely and earnestly seek love, peace, and the aid of this divine wisdom for its own sake, for the sake of spiritual healing, and for the sake of service to others. Seeking spiritual knowledge to wield power over others, to interfere with the life path and lessons of others, or to manipulate, coerce, or con in any way is a violation of the sacred spiritual law of free will and sovereignty.

We honor, respect, and protect our authority over our own soul force, and we must, in turn, honor, respect, and protect the authority others have over their soul force. Seek soul force's wisdom with humility. Serve yourself and humanity humbly. Integrate your spiritual lessons, learnings and revelations quietly. Remember, this divine connection is our relationship to cultivate and honor, and it is ours alone. We may feel compelled to share, discuss, and explore our experiences with family, friends, and neighbors, and this is a wonderful way to grow soul force within and with others, so long as the discourse is free, open, loving, nonjudgmental, and noncoercive. Remember, our experience of the divine will be what is true for us. It is not up to us to impose our experiences on others. This is never OK. Coercion of any kind violates the sacred spiritual law of free will and sovereignty we have all been blessed with.

As I mentioned earlier in this book, we are often the summation of the five people we spend the most time with, so I urge you to think of spending time with soul force as visiting a close friend whom you wish to spend more time with. In my experience, the more I allow myself to be in the still company of this healing vibration, the more the presence and prevalence of love, compassion, and wisdom remain with me as I move through the world, in both subtle and profound ways. Carving out time to sit with spirit can be challenging in our busy, day-to-day hustle. I feel a daily practice of fifteen or twenty quality minutes a day of uninterrupted meditation, prayer, silence, and focused contemplation with soul force can provide a tremendously transformative injection of higher love and wisdom into our experience.

Building on the practices introduced earlier, set aside fifteen or twenty minutes to connect to soul force. Find a quiet space at home, or better yet seek a space in nature, where life exists in its own organized, effortless, and peaceful way. Set an intention at the top of the meditation to connect with the pure soul force that is universal light and love before beginning your rhythmic breathing and the soul-force-field meditation. Once you've rooted yourself in Mother Earth with your grounding cord and the light of love surrounds you in your sacred meditative space, move briefly through each of the seven chakras, starting at the root chakra and moving up through the crown. This allows you to slowly raise your vibration from Earth to that of your soul force. When you get to the crown chakra, repeat a mantra of gratitude: "I am thankful to be alive and breathing. I am thankful for this divine connection. I am thankful for loving awareness."

Repeat this mantra as you allow the light of soul force to move into and through you. Be open to the sounds, images, sensations, and impressions that may arise as you enter into this holy union. If you are focused and open, it is not uncommon to have extrasensory experiences in this state. You may also experience nothing at all or perhaps stillness and transcendence. There is no right outcome to this exercise. The divine will manifest and appear as it should for you where you are on your spiritual journey and in that moment. The important thing is to keep your intention fixed on connecting to divine love. This keeps the vibration of your intention and destination aligned with the ultimate transcendent reality where we are safe, loved, and welcomed. When you are finished, thank soul force for the time, the space, and the connection. Express gratitude for the love and wisdom shared. Open your eyes. Take a deep breath.

Tell me, how does it feel to be connected to soul force?

DREAMING WITH SOUL FORCE

One of the easiest ways for soul force, our higher self, and our superconscious mind to communicate with us is in our sleep. When we're awake, our overanalytical, hypercritical, linear processing and judging mind constantly works in overdrive. This is a relatively normal state for a western mind, at least in my experience. When we are present in this type of consciousness, it is difficult to perceive more subtle sensations and impressions that we might otherwise pick up in a meditation or when quietly working with our chakras. Think of the difference between having a conversation with someone in a quiet room and having a conversation in the middle of a Metallica concert. The number of people and the amplified sounds alone would make it difficult to hear the person you're talking to or even focus on each other. Without training our mind how to focus in situations like this, there's simply too much sensory stimulation to be fully present and aware in the conversation with the person in front of you.

JEFF BOMBERGER

Our highest self, the part of us that is inseparable from soul force, communicates through high-frequency vibrations that are subtly perceptible in our auric energy fields; therefore, it can be very challenging to receive higher wisdom amid the incessant buzzing of ordinary reality without practice, time, attention, and proper training. At night, though, the whole world slows down, and everything gets quiet. Our mental and physical world grinds to a halt, and we finally lie down to rest. Suddenly, a vibrant and fluid world of possibilities emerge as we enter our dream state. Unbound by the laws of physics, convention, and society, the landscape of our dreams allows us to go anywhere, be anybody, and see, do, and experience just about anything imaginable. This nonordinary aspect of consciousness provides spirit the perfect canvas and palette through which symbols, lessons, and messages can be transmitted and shared with us our on journey through life.

Even with my own minor flashes of psychic phenomena as a kid, I was still relatively skeptical of psychic potential because I simply could not understand where the information came from or how it worked. When it came to dreams, though, there was logic present that made more sense to me. At minimum, I could rationalize that my dreams were some sort of manifestation of my deep subconscious mind. I knew that the subconscious mind is like a big hard drive that holds on to every experience we've ever had. Therefore, it made sense to me that in a time of restful sleep, manifestations of repressed thoughts, feelings, and emotions might emerge in some sort of a Jungian archetype that was representative of my hidden inner life. I didn't have to "prove" information was coming from somewhere outside of myself; dreams could simply be stories inspired by the emotions and energies percolating deep in my consciousness. I could safely accept this explanation as both useful and rational. As you can imagine, that theory was challenged when I had my dream about the United States' invasion of Iraq.

My dream life has been vibrant and active for as long as I can remember. My father, my mother, and my sister are all quite active dreamers as well, and analyzing our dreams was a practice my family got into regularly while at the dinner table. My dad really was the pioneer on this front of consciousness more than any of us, although curiously enough my dad never had dreams—at least not that he can remember—until he was in his early thirties. Then, one day, it was as if someone flipped a switch, and he suddenly began having vivid, memorable, and communicative dreams. The thing to know about my dad is he's got an engineering mind, in the sense that he's practical and all about tangible results. He loves making puzzle pieces fit together, both literally and figuratively. The onslaught of dream activity led him on his own spiritual quest to understand and make practical use of his dream life, and I have to give him a lot of credit for being an incredible teacher in this way.

In reality, I owe it to my whole family for creating a safe space to open up our dreamworlds to the possibility of seeking wisdom and insight in the magical mind movies that play out while we sleep. This process became extremely valuable for us on our own respective spiritual journeys because it allowed us to see ourselves, our emotions, and our life situations with more clarity at times. For example, a dream might cause us to look more deeply at our true feelings about something going on at school or work or clue us in to recognizing the emotional perspective of someone we're in relationship with. Most importantly, we came to see our dreams as mirrors, reflecting back to us aspects of ourselves we may not always see clearly in waking consciousness.

Engaging in this process together was incredibly fruitful, and, for our purposes here, provided an intimate, loving, and nonjudgmental forum for which we could begin to decipher the language of our souls together. Even though a lot of the symbolism in dreams relies on the specific relevance of each symbol to the individual dreamer, we've identified quite a few common archetypes that can help guide a dreamer toward deeper inner seeing. It is helpful on our soul-force journey to make an effort to extract meaning, wisdom, and insight from our dream state. I won't speak for everyone else in my family, but I will stand and give testament to the transformative power of being open to the information that may come through in dreams if we allow it. The bottom line is that our dream life—no matter where we may believe or imagine it comes from—does hold messages that can help us see more clearly, widen our aperture, heal, and at times unlock hidden potential.

This process of analyzing dreams for one another is still an ongoing practice in my family today. In fact, we regularly refer to my dad as "the dream master," and we tend to go to him first for his insights. This is because his now two decades of dream work have given us a treasure trove of experience and insight that allows us to see ourselves and the world through a wider spiritual perspective as we walk our paths of personal evolution. While I have had my own experiences signifying that spirit, spirit guides, and even loved ones who have crossed over can communicate with us in our dreams, for the sake of introducing you to the power of dreams, we won't venture into this expansive territory quite yet as there is much to learn as it relates to your very personal dream awareness alone. This leads us to taking the first step toward learning how to initiate dreaming with soul force.

How to Dream with Soul Force

Consciously setting the intention to receive messages and information in dreams is the most direct way to open up to this power within. The dream world is fantastic, strange, mystical, fluid, and complex, especially as we consciously wade into this realm for the first time. To begin dreaming with soul force, you're going to want to simply set the intention to do so. Before you go to bed at night, tell yourself that you want to remember your dreams from the night. This will signal the brain to pay attention and retain memory of wherever the mind may wander in your sleep state.

You'll also want to complement that gesture by getting into the habit of journaling what you remember of your dreams immediately the next morning. This habit is just as important as reminding the mind to remember your dreams in the first place. By immediately grabbing a pad and pen upon waking up, you leave little time for the conscious mind to kick in and begin to clutter your thoughts with appointments, meetings, and deadlines that may loom beyond your awakening. In these beginning stages of dreaming with soul force, you don't want to necessarily analyze your dreams yet. You simply want to get used to remembering what you dream. When you wake up and recall your dreams, start simple by recalling what time of day the dream took place. What was the setting and environment? Who was there? Are there any colors, smells, or sensations that stood out? Were there animals, symbols, or objects that left a particular impression? How did you feel in the dream? Scared, angry, confused, happy, excited? What was going on? What were you doing? Recall and write down as much information as you possibly can because even the smallest, most minute detail could hold a big key. When you get in this habit, you train the brain to pay attention to all these fine details, both when you're dreaming and when you're awake.

Once you've developed a routine of journaling and you're recalling more and more of your dream life, then you can start to move into general dream interpretations. When you get to this stage, start your morning by writing down your dream, and then reflect on the general impression the dream made on you. Don't get too nitty-gritty about the details and what they mean at first; go with significant impressions, thoughts, and feelings that stand out or stick with you overall. How did the dream make you feel? Who or what did the dream remind you of? When you first check in, what are the three most significant initial impressions, feelings, or vibes that you get from the dream? For example, was it dark, rainy, and unfamiliar? Were you surrounded by people you know but felt alone anyway? Begin the journey with dream analysis here in a more general and broad way. As I mentioned, dreaming with soul force is like learning a new language. It's going to take time, immersion, and repetition before you start to notice patterns and begin to intuit the messages they hold for you.

JEFF BOMBERGER

As you build up a log of dreams, start to take notice of any patterns in your dream life. As best you can, try to connect the dots of any signs, symbols, and themes that are reoccurring. Don't be afraid to turn to your meditative practice and chakra work to seek clarity on what is coming through for you. As your dream life grows and your aptitude for remembering, sensing, feeling, and intuiting your dreams increases, take the plunge into trying to dissect the details a little bit further. Here's where the puzzle piecing really begins.

For the sake of returning to our soul force and getting in touch with our true essence, we (meaning my dad and I) have compiled this short list of signs and symbols that can help launch you on your quest to understanding messages your soul force may be trying to send you in your sleep. Not all dreams hold deep and profound spiritual, emotional, or even physical messages. A lot of times they can be connected to mundane, day-to-day feelings and experiences. Also, not all dreams are literal. In fact, often dreams fall into the category of being symbolic and archetypal because the messages deal with lessons related to our spiritual growth. When it comes to our spiritual path, an important part of the journey is consciously awakening, and living experiences and acquiring wisdom. This means we will rarely "get" the exact answers we're looking for in plain and simple form because it robs us of the conscious realization we're meant to come by. We have found that when a dream is communicating a particularly important spiritual message, the dream experience tends to be vivid and visceral and often bears a unique weight. You will need to do your own work in figuring out how your dreams speak to you as well as how they feel when they resonate as important or true, which is another great reason to keep a dream journal over time.

While the great majority of the dreams I've discussed and shared with my family remain in the symbolic realm, I have also had my share of dreams that very literally reveal to me a particular aspect of reality. You may also have this experience, so don't rule it out. These types of dreams, for me, are far less frequent than the others, but they leave a very distinct impression on me and, at this point in my experience, tend to be related to matters beyond my personal experience. For what reason these dreams come, I have yet to come to a satisfactory conclusion. My awareness of these kinds of impressions grew with time, with experience, and with recognition of their very distinct feel. You too may have experiences like these, and it is going to be up to you to learn the language of your dreams, through trial, error, and pure direct experience.

The analyses and descriptions below have been put together to assist you with developing a rudimentary dream language so that you can understand the symbolic dreams you're likely to experience. These breakdowns are not the be-all and end-all of dream-life interpretation, and we could very well fill an entire book on just dream analysis and dream symbols as we've come to understand them. Like everything else in this material, check in with how our suggestions resonate with you and your intuition. Take what works and discard what doesn't. Be courageous in your own pursuit of knowledge and wisdom. Most importantly, remember to set the intention to remember your dreams!

Basic Dream Symbols to Build On

The symbols below have been broken up into basic categories, but it is important to note that they aren't mutually exclusive. The language of dreams requires us to look at how all the pieces of the puzzle come together to paint a coherent picture for us to analyze.

For example, say you have a dream that takes place at nighttime, inside your childhood home. You're trying to fix a plumbing leak in the kitchen while your mother watches and tells you not to worry about it. You keep trying and trying to stop the leak until finally the pipe bursts, the kitchen floods, and the feeling is yuck!

This relatively simple dream is loaded with clues directing our attention at where to look if we want to extract meaning from the dream. In short, if you came to me with this dream, my instinct would be to look at how

AWAKENING SOUL FORCE

your mom influenced your capacity to handle yucky emotions and if her influence has led to an inability to adequately keep small emotional issues from becoming too overwhelming.

In breaking the symbolism down, we immediately have to acknowledge the presence of Mom, as her energy and influence is connected to the message of the dream. You're in a childhood home, so we want to look at your formative years. The kitchen is in your parent's house, so technically it is Mom's kitchen, the place where she feeds you, so we're going to look at how she, specifically, created space to nourish you. Water in dreams tends to represent emotions, and since the water in your dream was yucky, I'd say we'd want to take a deeper look at the childhood environment Mom created for you as it relates to handling negative emotions.

This dream is hinting that Mom's dismissive or nonchalant attitude toward seemingly minor matters of negative emotion has subconsciously influenced you to be less equipped to manage any excess negative emotions yourself. Water leaking from the normally hidden pipes is symbolic of hidden emotions that are not draining properly and spilling out where they are not supposed to be. The dream shows us that this inability to fix the problem ultimately leads you to be overwhelmed and flooded by a burst of yucky emotion.

Finally, because the dream takes place at night, this

would indicate to me this is likely an influence you may not be consciously aware of as nighttime often refers to aspects of our unconscious or subconscious mind. The dream is, in reality, a vehicle for you to recognize these elements and bring them into your awareness so that you may heal them appropriately. This is the power of dream analysis, and I hope you'll find the following introductory guide to dream symbols helpful on your quest to connecting to your transformative soul force within.

Daytime

During the daytime, light shines on everything in our conscious awareness. Dreams that take place during the day often reflect activity, energy, and emotion present in our conscious life. The symbolism of these dreams often reflects qualities, aspects, issues, and behaviors we are aware of. Daytime dreams may also be indicative of hopes, dreams, and aspirations as well as serve as a reflection of where we're going or would like to be.

Nighttime

At night, we roam in the mystery of the dark unknown and unseen. Dreams that take place during the nighttime often reflect the activity, energy, and emotion that resides in the unconscious and subconscious mind. Their influences may subtly inform actions and behaviors we display out in the world but are, ultimately, rooted beneath the surface; therefore, we have to dig a little deeper to see these aspects of ourselves more clearly. Pitch-black skies and extreme darkness in dreams may also be pointing to fears and anxieties that consciously and subconsciously have a grip on us.

Water

Water typically has to do with emotions, but can also be connected to creativity. How that water manifests in a dream can be reflective of the intensity of emotions we are sensing or feeling, both consciously and subconsciously. How and where water appears can also be important in recognizing what message the dream has for us. In deciphering whether or not the water in your dream relates to creativity or emotion, you'll want to look at the other elements present in your dream and, ultimately, your relationship to the water itself. How do you feel about the water in the dream? What is the quality of the water? Is it refreshing? Overwhelming? What is the general sense you feel in relationship with the water?

Water can manifest in many different forms, each of which may be a clue as to which aspects of your creativity and emotions are being expressed in the dream. Water within piping under the sink, in the walls, or under the ground has to do with aspects that are hidden or out of sight.

An ocean has to do with big emotions. Big waves,

high swells, and things that overwhelm are reflective of tumultuous, rocky emotions that are difficult to navigate. On the contrary, still and calm waters are indicators of feelings of contentment and being at ease and in a "good place" and can also be reflective of emotions that are manageable and easy to navigate.

Swimming in a pool at home can be reflective of emotions related to our home life and family or an emotional space we share with others. Swimming in a public pool can be related to emotions we experience interacting with the public at large. Water in a bathtub will have to do with more personal and intimate emotions, those we experience in private.

Rain and snow are also manifestations of water. The quality of rain or snow holds key insights into the quality of emotions we are being asked to look at. A torrential downpour can be indicative of emotions that get dumped on us, while a light drizzle may reflect us navigating a lighter, less overwhelming emotional environment.

Ice and snow have to do with cold, hardened, or frozen emotions. Ice and snow can be frigid, dangerous, cumbersome, and even paralyzing, or they can be playgrounds to be enjoyed via ice skates, skis, and snowboards. How we interact with the ice and snow can turn us on to how we relate to these emotions.

Fire

Fire is representative of passion and/or anger as well as the transformative quality of spirit, depending on the context of the dream. Like water, it's important to look to your own feelings about fire and what the fire in your dream inspires in you. Does the fire torch all in its path and inspire fear or relief? Feeling relief from the destruction of a fiery blaze could indicate a welcome change. Feeling fear could indicate resistance to change. If we actually feel heat or pressure from the fire in our dream, this may be related to a more personal experience of inflamed passions or anger, as the temperature of the flames affects us personally. A fire in our home may be guiding us to look at the quality of passion, anger, or spirit in relation to our physically contained self. A fire from the outside, threatening our home, may be related to passion, anger, and transformative forces converging on us from the outside world.

Houses and Rooms

Our home is our space, our private world. It is where we reside; therefore, dreaming inside a particular house is reflective of the self. When we dream of activity inside our house, we're being directed to look at the behavior, energy, and influences present in who we are and how they relate to the integrity of self. Dreaming of the front yard is pointing us toward looking at our public facing self, while the back yard is a more private place to interact with and entertain friends, family, and other loved ones.

Dreams that take place in our childhood home direct our attention to the formative years of our life. Activity, energy, emotion, and behavior explored in the dream will likely be rooted in experiences from childhood. They often require us to look more closely at how those experiences are influencing and manifesting themselves in our lives right now.

The living room is where we put our feet up, relax, and share space with those closest to us. Dreams that take place in the living room can be related to energy and behavior when we feel most comfortable and at home. There are also elements of how we relate to others when we welcome them in and entertain or host people in our intimate space.

The kitchen is where we cook food. The dining table is where we eat. Fundamentally, these are the places we feed ourselves. Dreams that take place in the kitchen or dining areas are related to physical, emotional, and energetic nourishment. They are related to our consumption—what we're being fed, so to speak, and how what we're being fed is prepared for us or by us.

When we are upstairs in a home, we are exploring a higher level of awareness. Therefore, dreams that take place upstairs in a home or on upper floors of a building are related to higher aspects of the mind and the intellect as well as our higher self and things we are consciously aware of.

When we are in the basement of a home, we are exploring matters that exist below the surface. Therefore, dreams that take place in basements are often related to things we have not consciously realized, aspects of our subconscious mind, and the energies and emotions that exist under the external, public self.

Our bedroom is our most private room, our most intimate and innermost space. It is where we are most vulnerable and where we share personal intimacy. Dreams that relate to the bedroom direct us to look at our most private thoughts, feelings, energy, and behaviors.

The shower or bathtub is where we cleanse ourselves, and it is our most intimate interaction with water. Therefore, dreams that take place in the shower or bathtub can often point us toward the way we process and handle intimate emotions, cleanse ourselves, and wash away energetic muck.

The toilet is where we relieve ourselves and get rid of emotional and physical waste. Dreams about using the toilet direct us to look at how we relieve ourselves of unneeded and unnecessary people, places, energy, and emotions.

Being Naked

When we are naked, we are stripped down bare—vulnerable and, at the same time, free. Dreaming of being naked can reflect the true nature of who we are. Being naked in dreams can also shine a light on our relationship to who we are and how we feel about being vulnerable and, ultimately, free. It's important to note how we feel in the dream when naked. Are we casually strolling about? Are we embarrassed? Are we confident? Are we ashamed? Looking at how we feel in relation to being naked will give us a clue as to how we may be feeling exposed in one way or another.

Clothing

Clothing has much to do with how we appear in the world and how we present ourselves. When we dream of clothes, how they fit, what they look like, if they are changing, coming off, or piling on, these symbols can point us to looking more closely at how we're presenting ourselves to the world.

Hair

Hair grows and flows from our head. When the focal point of a dream is around hair, it is directing us toward our thoughts. Hair color can be reflective of the quality of our thoughts, whether growing darker, lighter, vibrant, or changing hues. The length and texture of our hair—whether it is long or short, tangled or straight—are also symbols reflecting back at us the kind of thoughts we have. Long, flowing hair can represent filled out thoughts and wisdom, whereas short hair could represent simpler, tighter thoughts. Straight, easy-to-work-with hair can indicate thoughts that are cooperative and manageable, while tangled hair may indicate confusion or thoughts that are difficult to manage. Sometimes we may dream of our hair being cut. Who is cutting our hair? Is it being reshaped, trimmed, or lopped off? Getting our hair cut is about shaping our thoughts. We also may dream about losing our hair, which is a shedding of thoughts, releasing them, and letting them go.

Teeth

Teeth help us break down food into digestible pieces. Therefore, teeth are often connected to our ability to process and break down that which feeds or nourishes us. Losing teeth or having teeth fall out can often reflect a shift, change, or transformation in the way we process what we welcome into our life as nourishment.

Vehicles

Vehicles represent the ways in which we move through the world and how we get to where we are trying to go. Cars are our personal vehicles and the way we get around. Symbols and issues surrounding our car tend to reflect the spiritual and physical self. Not being able to find the keys to our car may indicate an inability to find what we need to get ourselves going on a particular path. A car with foggy windows might indicate a difficulty seeing where we are going. Someone else driving our car may represent an aspect of ourselves that has taken the wheel, so to speak, on our journey.

Boats are used to navigate water, which we've already established is representative of emotions. Therefore, boats represent our ability to handle emotional situations. A surfboard is a youthful and energetic way to ride waves. Dreaming of being tossed around in an inflatable raft may indicate a less dynamic way of moving through emotions (although it does float). A pirate ship may indicate a rebellious approach to navigating waters, whereas a cruise ship may be reflecting an organization or group of people moving through waters in a more public context.

Airplanes fly through the air and take us on bigger journeys. Therefore, planes tend to represent larger personal, emotional, or spiritual trips and how we get there. Being a passenger on a plane may direct us to look at the travels that we have no control over, while actually piloting the plane might direct us to look at our ability to navigate this trip ourselves. A commercial airplane is likely representative of a more collective experience, while a small biplane would represent a more personal journey.

Motorcycles are more individually focused, adaptable, and exposed modes of transportation. There's more risk and more danger in riding them but with that comes more freedom. A dirt bike may represent a more youthful, playful, and adventurous way of moving through the world or a road less traveled. A street bike is made for speed and can make for skipping traffic along conventional roads and highways. A Harley is more of a cruiser used on open roads and longer journeys.

Skateboards and scooters are other alternative and more experimental ways of moving through the world. They bring in youthful energy, flexibility, and adaptability.

Having our mode of transportation break down or become dysfunctional may indicate that the way in which we're navigating the world has rendered us stuck or stagnant or simply is not working for us anymore.

Accidents can point us to meeting something unexpectedly on our journey or something we don't see coming or may even indicate a sudden change in our travels.

Roads and Bridges

Roads are pathways that help us get from point A to point B. The condition of the roads and the environment around them can all hold symbolic meaning for us, depending on what journey we're moving along at a particular point in our life.

Bridges typically carry us over some sort of obstacle and join pieces of land that are otherwise not connected. Bridges can represent synthesis, transitions, and movement between distinct or seemingly unrelated parts of our journey.

People

People in our dreams can be a little tricky. In many cases, the people we dream of are symbols, just like the rest of the imagery we've explored. When it comes to figuring out who the people in our dreams represent and what their role is in the message, we have to look more at the energy, essence, and qualities of the person than the physical body we're seeing in order to find the answers.

Typically, when you see someone you know in real life in your dream, you'll want to look at the qualities, essence, and energy of that person. Having your mother, father, brother, sister, friend, or coworker present in the dream can represent the influence of their energy on the situation being explored. They could also represent a part of you that is similar to them that is being reflected back to you. When you think of the person in your dream, what are the first three words that come to mind? When you answer that question, you can then look to either the aspect of yourself that reflects these qualities or someone else in your life who shares these qualities.

For example, my sister often pops up in my dreams

as the representation of my feminine nature. I once had a rather revelatory dream about my relationship to my pain and suffering, specifically as it relates to my willingness to acknowledge pain in close relationships. The dream took place in the backyard of my childhood home, and I witnessed a pack of rabid domestic dogs attack my brilliant-white pet wolf. When they first attacked him, I hesitated to jump in and defend him because I didn't want them to attack me. It looked like he was going to be OK, but then suddenly my white wolf split open and collapsed. Instead of rendering aid, my first instinct was to run inside the house and make sure I shielded my sister's eyes from the bloodshed. So I ran into the house and hung solid-white curtains so she could not see my dying wolf in the backyard.

When I think of my sister, the first three words that pop into my mind are *sensitive, compassionate,* and *selfless*. Because this dream took place in the backyard of my childhood home and revolved around my white wolf, I knew this dream was focused on me. Therefore, I assumed my sister was a reference to the part of myself that is sensitive, compassionate, and selfless. Breaking all the symbols down, I recognized that I'd developed a habit of using my spirituality (white curtains) to shield myself from fully confronting the pain I'd feel when those close to me assaulted my purest nature (my white wolf). Afraid to intervene and "save" my highest pure instincts, I would instead go into my house—in other words, go inward—and put up a blinding wall of white so that the sensitive, compassionate, and selfless part of myself would not have to deal with the pain and horror of feeling "attacked." As you can imagine, this was a real wake-up call for me when I connected these dots to what I was experiencing in my real life.

When we see and interact with people in our dreams who we don't personally know in our waking life, like celebrities or movie characters, for instance, these can also be hidden or unfamiliar aspects of ourselves relating back to us. They can also be indicative of a person close to us who exhibits similar qualities. Using the same trick of naming the first three traits that come to mind when we think of the person appearing in our dream, we can decipher what aspects of ourselves the dream is bringing to light. These mysterious and hidden qualities of self can be great teachers for us if we remain open minded and objective about how we view their relationship to us in our dream experience.

For example, let's say you dream of the *Game of Thrones* character Daenerys Targaryen, Mother of Dragons, telling you she's thirsty and needs water. Sounds random, right? Well, what are the first three personal qualities that come to mind for you when you think of her? To me, Daenerys embodies the empowered feminine, strength, and freedom. If I dreamed of her, I'd look to either the feminine aspect of myself that embodied those qualities or look to a woman in my life—say, my partner—who to me does embody similar qualities of strength, freedom, and feminine power. She's thirsty and looking for water, which symbolically would tell me she's looking for emotional fulfillment or nourishment. If I then take this message and apply it to my life, I may discover one of two things: either there are feminine qualities in myself that need creative and/or emotional nourishment, or my partner is in need of emotional love and support.

The magic of the dreamworld is that so much of the language can be understood and deciphered by us universally, yet at the end of the day, it always comes back to the experience of the dreamer and what the symbols mean to them personally. What does Daenerys mean to you? If you had the dream above, how might you interpret it based on your own conceptions and definitions? Chances are you may come up with something varied or slightly different than what I offered, and that's great. Answering those questions for yourself puts you on the path to deciphering the language of dreaming with soul force on your own!

Finally, as it relates to people, dreams of being pregnant or having babies can point to new beginnings in your life that are happening or are coming down the pipeline. Babies are a by-product of our fundamental ability to create, and when they arrive—whether as actual children or something else that wants to be birthed through us—we must nurture them, care for them, and help them grow.

Animals

Animals in dreams tend to relate to aspects and qualities within ourselves. Dogs tend to represent our more basic instinctual urges and a primal masculine nature. Cats tend to represent our intuitive instincts and the primal feminine nature. Birds tend to represent our more innate spiritual instincts and our spiritual nature.

The definitions and breakdowns above are barely scratching the surface of the wonder of dream life. Hopefully, these basic definitions can provide you with some tools to help you look at and analyze your dreams with a more curious and insightful eye. It is also important for you to become your own inner explorer. Seek clarity in your meditations and chakra work and trust your own intuitions around what you find. The value of engaging in the process of dream analysis is that it allows us to see our inner life through more objective and nonjudgmental eyes. Viewing ourselves and the ebb and flow of our energy from a place of loving awareness creates space for us to heal and transform energy, wounds, and relationships more quickly than if we left our conscious mind to simply figure it out. Dreams are a nonordinary

AWAKENING SOUL FORCE

aspect of reality, a space where we can have profound direct experience of our inner world without intellectual blockages. With this broader perspective and clearer vision, we then have the freedom to more consciously transform ourselves and live a life in greater awareness of the workings of soul force.

HEALING WITH SOUL FORCE

A powerful capability at our disposal is the ability to heal ourselves through our connection to pure soul force. By engaging in the process of rhythmic breathing, as well as balancing and revitalizing your chakras, you have already been dabbling in the arena of self-healing with soul-force energy. In fact, this entire process of undoing what the world has done to you is, in and of itself, a transformative healing process. We are going to take this ability one step further by exploring a healing meditation you may employ on yourself in any and all circumstances for which you need to heal the physical body.

This technique is a wonderful preventative practice as well as a supplement to any kind of medical care that you should seek in the case of compromised wellness. Self-energy healing is not a replacement for modern medicine. The power of self-healing truly lies in fixating your mind-set on the feeling, sensation, and belief in healing, wholeness, and wellness. We've spent a great deal of time attuning our attention and awareness to the vibration of healing and love, which transforms our own energy. This healing meditation is meant to help attune the physical body to a state of wellness, even when it temporally experiences a state of injury or disease.

Either lying down or sitting in a chair (whichever is more comfortable for you), use rhythmic breathing to center yourself and prepare for self-healing. After a few rounds of rhythmic breathing, call in divine white light, love, and protection. You may ask for the love and protection of your highest creator throughout this meditation as it will be the source of healing. Then imagine the ball of white light springing from the crown of your head, and watch it roll down your spine until it links up with the tip of your tail bone. Imagine a white cord extending from the tip of your tail bone, and send that sturdy cord down to the center of the earth. This is your energetic grounding cord.

Wiggle your toes, and imagine your feet merging with the soil. Then visualize thick reddish-brown roots growing out of your feet and running deep into the earth. This is you connecting to the energy and vibration of Mother Earth. In return, she sends a beautiful vibrant orange light up through the roots and into your body. This light travels up your ankles, your legs, your torso, and out the top of your head and then encircles you in a big, vibrant orange energy bubble.

Now imagine the deepest night sky above you, sprinkled with twinkling starlight. When you're ready, imagine the sky parting and a luminous white light shining

AWAKENING SOUL FORCE

down from this opening, into the top of your head, right in the center of your crown. This light enters the spinal cord through your head and runs down your neck, shoulders, torso, legs, and all the way through the soles of your feet. When it comes out the bottom, this white light also forms a luminous bubble all around you. Sit in this light for a moment, thanking your Creator for the divine light, love, and protection. Then state your intention for this meditation: to balance and heal your body.

Next, imagine breathing in the divine white light you've connected to. With each inhale, imagine feeling the sensation of high vibrational, healing energy moving in through your nose, down into your lungs, then into your heart and circulatory system. Feel this white light traveling throughout your entire body through the blood vessels. As you exhale, imagine any dark, muddy, and cloudy energy being expelled out the grounding cord and being sucked down into the center of the earth to be absorbed. Repeat this visualization until you've allowed white light to fill your entire body and all of your extremities. Continue this pattern over and over until you've expelled all negative energy out of your body.

Once you're filled with white light and you've expelled all the negative energy in your body, imagine a detailed image of your body as it sits or lies. In your mind's eye, picture a pair of healing hands, glowing white with a hint of green, above you. Now turn your attention to any area of your body where you may be experiencing an injury, physical pain, trauma, or disease. Direct those healing hands to the affected area, and imagine the warm, loving, healing sensation of these hands resting on this area. Once the healing hands are comfortably in place, give thanks for the energy remedy by repeating the mantra "I am thankful for this healing."

Repeat this over and over to yourself or aloud, whatever feels most comfortable. As you repeat the mantra, imagine the white and green healing light moving into your cells and making them whole again. If you have a broken bone, imagine the bone piecing itself back together, cell by cell, until it is whole. If you're experiencing inflammation, imagine the tension and inflammation being calmed by this healing light and the tissue returning to a normal state. Whatever the ailment, visualize your fully healed body, and direct the energy toward restoring your body to this state of optimum health and well-being. Remain focused on repeating this mantra and visualization for as long as you see necessary.

When you're finished with the healing session, thank the divine healing hands once more for the time and healing. Share your gratitude for the chance to be alive and breathing. Share your gratitude for the opportunity to heal and be healed. Before you open your eyes, take a few more deep breaths in through your nose and out your mouth, circulating healing energy and making sure any excess negative energy is expelled into the earth. When you feel purified and ready, you may open your eyes and conclude your self-healing session.

AUTOMATIC WRITING
WITH SOUL FORCE

July 20, 2016

Beloved Jeffrey, keep yourself elevated. Don't let your thoughts get bogged down with should and should nots. There is no such thing as should. There is only what you wish to experience. Move into that. Remember, you have come to the space to heal the space. Wherever you show up, there you are. And so, too, is your divine consciousness and connection. Your awakening is the world's awakening. Be awake. That is all. And by simply being, your presence awakens and stirs the "you" inside of others. You being close to love brings everyone closer to love.

It is about presence. Do not do. Do not try. Simply show up and be. There is no other requirement. Focus on your awakening. Strengthen your connection. Be close to source. And when you feel you should go into the world or go into the community, do just that. Remember, inspirations are suggestions. They are not hard truths. They aren't finite directions.

JEFF BOMBERGER

They are merely suggestions. No one is here to tell you what to do but you. No one creates your life for you, but others can create life with you, based on you what you desire on a soul level.

Masters are among you. Teachers are all around you. They are present always. Masters and teachers look, speak, act and appear in an infinite variety of ways. Which best reflects you? Do you see the beauty of this game? You write the rules. You steer the ship. You call the shots. How do you wish to appear? Then be just that! In all its glory, nuance and ambiguity. Be all that you are. Let the world see all your faces, all your incarnations. Only you can determine what that looks like.

I appreciate you coming here. I appreciate your commitment to higher learning and deeper understanding. This is only the beginning of what is in store for you. Please move fully into your heart and go where it leads you. Speak, write, act and "think" with your heart awareness. This is your connection to love.

The channeled writing above comes from one of my many personal automatic writing sessions I've conducted over the years. I feel that this message very lovingly and simply captures the essence of what inspired me to write this material that you hold in your hands now. Remove my name from the letter, insert your name, and turn your awareness to how this message resonates with you. Now read the passage again. How does that feel? For me, personally, I feel inspired and reassured by the clarity and wisdom that comes alive through this message. It transcends the intellect, cuts through layers of semantics, and gets right to the heart of the matter. It all seems so simple. With this chapter, I hope to help open you up to the possibility of connecting to this clearer perspective and higher wisdom that is awaiting within you.

When I was a teenager, I began experimenting with the practice known as automatic writing. The practice is akin to freewriting or stream-of-consciousness writing, but it involves entering into a meditative state prior to putting pen to paper. My earliest recollection of dabbling with the technique goes back to when I was seventeen—a couple of years after I began meditating. This was also a year before I came across Neale Donald Walsch's *Conversations with God* series, which are books created through automatic writing sessions. I remember how my early experiences brought insightful guidance that carried a calmness and reassurance through my handwritten words. I continued the activity on and off throughout the years, and nearly all automatic writings I've ever completed sit in stacks of yellow legal pads that date back to the early 2000s.

Early on, I found myself automatic writing most frequently in times of mental confusion or emotional turmoil. *Conversations with God* served as an inspiration for me to continue seeking my own deeper connection to higher wisdom and my higher self. In my late teens and early twenties, the technique served as a tool of convenience when I couldn't see the forest for the trees. My automatic writing sessions never failed to quell my anxieties and ease my tensions. For that fact alone, I've always been thankful for the practice, regardless of where I imagined the information to be coming from. As I grew older, I found myself being called more and more to my legal pads to sit and write. Over time, the practice shifted from my asking probing existential questions to my feeling an overwhelming sense that I needed to be quiet and listen. Eventually, I found myself receiving words of guidance and inspiration from a loving awareness that I could tune into most clearly in total silence.

After years of seeking guidance when I felt lost, I eventually felt like a higher perspective was seeking after me to push me along my spiritual development. In 2016, the impulse to get quiet, sit, and let the pen flow grew unflinchingly strong. My automatic writing sessions became more frequent and at times more complex and exponentially expansive. Through this work, I am beginning to see more and more of the big picture and the role that every human being on the planet has to play in the spiritual evolution of humanity.

This is going to be achieved through the spiritual

work of every single individual on this planet. Most significantly, the evolution of our species depends on those of us who have already answered or are feeling the call of soul force inviting us to go even deeper. Access to higher dimensions of consciousness and our most fundamental soul force is more available today than it has ever been in the history of humanity. If you sincerely and honestly wish to connect to the vibrant loving awareness at the core of you and all of creation, now is the perfect time to reach out and establish such a connection. When you do this, you invite peace, love, and truth directly into your heart, and when you integrate these qualities and characteristics into your awareness and your life, you are then granted an opportunity to manifest these ideals and these vibrations in physical form. For you to potentially do so in the most authentic and unique way, I encourage you to see if the automatic writing technique works for you.

I find this technique works best for me in total silence or with the subtle sounds of solfeggio frequencies in the background. Solfeggio frequencies make up the ancient six-tone musical scale that has been used in sacred music, chants, and hymns for centuries past. These spiritual frequencies have been helpful in raising my own vibration with sound, and they may also serve your healing well. Set the mood with these tones, or sit in total silence and perform a crown-chakra meditation.

Take yourself through the visualizations of using the grounding cord to connect to Earth, then connecting to divine light and asking for protection. Once you've done that, tune into the crown chakra by repeating this mantra: "I honor the divine and the divine in me."

When you feel connected, ask if there are any messages of love and guidance available for you to receive from higher wisdom. You may also set the intention to receive guidance from loving awareness and then begin asking questions you seek answers to. From there, simply keep your mind clear, put your pen to paper, and begin to let consciousness flow through you. Whatever comes to mind, let it flow freely and effortlessly onto the page. Don't worry about spelling or grammar, although in my experience the spelling is remarkably sharp when I'm in a meditative state. When you are finished writing, close the session by giving thanks for the message that came through. Go back and read what was channeled and see how it resonates with you.

Remember, this is just another tool in the spiritual toolbox that allows us to reclaim our soul authority. At minimum, this technique can unlock wisdom and secrets hidden deep within our subconscious mind. If the teachings of mystics, ancient wisdom, the expansive world of energy, and spirituality have anything to do with this, then we may find automatic writing to be a helpful practice for our own direct spiritual revelation. It

AWAKENING SOUL FORCE

is of the utmost importance to honor a pure intention to connect to soul force, to truth, and to love when doing this. If you are using this journey to become famous or to show off or to tell people you're more enlightened than them, then your intentions are not pure and you must abandon the material until you're sincerely ready to be free from the temptations of ego. This path is about you and your personal responsibility to connect to, nurture, and grow soul force from the inside out. After all, you are your soul authority.

WE ARE SOUL FORCE

You are soul force in motion. I am soul force in motion. Together, we are soul force in motion. I cannot begin to express the gratitude I feel knowing you have made it through the entirety of this material. Thank you for entertaining the thoughts, suggestions, and exercises I've shared with you on this journey. Nothing lights me up more than a dialogue and exchange of ideas that propel us toward a more intimate relationship with our higher self, God, the universe, our divine Creator, and the powerful soul force within us. Each and every one of us is both a child of God and a living expression of God. Each and every one of us is a healer in need of healing, here to heal ourselves and others in our own ways. Each and every one of us brings a unique and dynamic lens through which we view, experience, and express the soul-force energy that animates us all. By living our truth, walking in awareness, and breathing life into the higher ideals of peace, love, freedom, and wisdom, we are on the way to building a better world for all.

This new world is waiting to be born, and it yearns to be realized through you. It is my most sincere belief that you were meant to read these words and engage in this exchange of energy so that we can build up our capacity to be the most authentic, intuitive, compassionate, and loving force we can be in this world. It is our responsibility to realize the peaceful, free, and abundant energy within us so that love and creativity can be born into the world through us. The love embodied by soul force is peaceful and powerful. It is clear and compassionate. It is nonjudgmental and discerning. It is equitable and just, rational and orderly. Most of all, soul force is healing. It is the life force of nature that exists within and all around us and makes us whole individuals. When we return to this force within and become familiar with and honor its vibration, we may realize a renewed and revitalized existence in our lives and on this beautiful planet.

We have an unlimited ability to live a more intuitive life, connected to our highest wisdom, right now. So long as we hold a sincere and genuine intention to connect with our innermost truth, love, and the divine, we can access higher wisdom, attain metaphysical insight, and experience personal healing for ourselves. Our world is going through a rapid transformation as we inch closer toward the vibration of love and oneness that has been celebrated by all of the world's spiritual traditions. Each and every single person who awakens to soul force raises the vibration of humanity for oneself and for

AWAKENING SOUL FORCE

all. The stronger our personal connection to soul force, the more accessible higher wisdom and healing are for every human being on the planet. Therefore, it is up to each and every single one of us who feels the call to deepen our spiritual connection to answer this call and open up to the gift of transcendence that awaits not just us but all of humanity.

In today's materialist world, it is easy to lose sight of how to exist in alignment with our highest spiritual values. When we do, we fail to coexist in a way that is unified by our shared destiny of creating life on this Earth together in a beautiful cosmic collaboration. Instead, we fight, we scrap, and we scrape, in constant battle with perceived adversaries, failing to confront the biggest and only true adversary that exists: a loss of our spiritual self. We must be vigilant in our quest to stay awake and fend off the malaise of spiritual amnesia. Although it can be difficult to imagine being at peace with one another, remember that we must first master being at peace with ourselves. We cannot allow our inner life to be divorced from our outer life. We cannot let a hypermaterialized existence drain our flesh of the magic of spirit and strip our spirit of the joy of being in body. Our holy union as one people inhabiting the planet Earth cannot be allowed to be divided and segregated by ego's grandest delusions. Whenever we feel this divorce between ourselves and others, our highest truth, and how we live, we must refocus our attention on the unifying and unyielding truth of our soul force within.

Authority figures of all kinds will continue to tug at our attention, begging us to live our lives in accordance with values that conform to their materialistic agendas, fractured political ideologies, and profit-driven courses of action. These forces will attempt to direct us on what to buy, what to say, what to do, who to follow, what to think, and how to live. While at times and in moments, these so-called leaders may strike a chord somewhere near our true nature of loving awareness, we must remain centered in our own moral authority, higher wisdom, and deeper purpose. As a society, many will continue to search because what we truly seek is not outside of us but, rather, within. Therefore, the words of authority figures and the paternalistic approval of those who "know better" will always inevitably exist as a barrier between us and our own inner light, the pure soul force within. Again, it is up to us to sit with this inner light, nurture it, and grow it into the persistent and powerful force of love that it is.

Awakening to and living this transformative soul force is a call I've answered. Twenty years after my first experience with psychic phenomenon, I'm answering a call to help others to join me in living out this soul force within. I've set a lifetime intention to return to this most fundamental, pure, authentic spiritual self and strive to breathe physical life into its vibration every single day. I hope you too will find the passion and the courage to seek the highest expression of love within you. It is my soul's deepest wish to free myself and others from the throes of ego, the anguish of suffering, and the delusions of a violent, traumatic world so that we can breathe new life into ourselves and, as a result, give rise to a sturdy vibration of love on this planet. I've long been on a quest, seeking my innermost voice, my own loving awareness, and my most authentic spiritual vibration, and the journey continues on through the writing of this material and beyond.

It is my most heartfelt hope that our time together inspired more questions than answers. I hope you have found the material in your hands to be compelling, thought provoking, enlightening, and in some way healing. My soul motivation is to inspire you to continue to pursue spiritual truth and direct revelation and to find pathways into your own most vibrant soul force in those ways that resonate as true and honest for you. I'm hoping my experiences and the tools I've shared provided insight, inspiration, and comfort on your own journey. For me, this book has been an expression of my own deep inner longing for us as an entire people to truly be free. Free to heal. Free to love. Free to evolve, innovate, and cooperate. Free to live a life empowered by our intuition, higher reason, and boundless creativity.

JEFF BOMBERGER

Most of all, I long for us to be free to live in loving awareness with ourselves and others. I want to realize this powerful energy within and walk in the beauty of its light. I want you to realize and demonstrate this powerful energy within you so that you can dream impossible dreams and achieve impossible things for yourself and the world you most intimately touch. More than anything, I wish for us to achieve a level of spiritual self-mastery and awareness that allows us be our own spiritual authority, faithfully walking in alignment with our own unique expression of loving soul force. For if we do that, our transformation will be the world's transformation. Our freedom will be the world's freedom. Our love will be the world's love.

Remember, be kind to yourself and others on this journey. We are all one. Live and speak your truth. Live and speak it powerfully, but live and speak it gently. Life itself is a practice. Walking in awareness is a practice. Healing is a process. Existence itself is an ongoing transformation. We are all on a path to loving awareness, in our own time and our own way—all in divine timing. Let us bless the path that got us here. Let us bless the here and now as much as we bless the bright and beautiful future ahead. I wish us all well on our endeavors and hope that our individual paths may cross in real time and in real space someday soon. I look forward to experiencing the impact of our shared growth, our shared freedom, and our shared prosperity together.

Now is the time for a transformative shift in human consciousness on a mass scale. We have to plant the seeds for expanded self-awareness and higher dimensions of consciousness so they may grow over the next five, ten, fifteen, twenty to one hundred years into the sturdy pillars of wisdom our culture must grow to stand on. The next phase of our journey together will be *Living with Soul Force*, where we will continue to deepen our connection to soul force and our highest self as well dive deep into all forms of the divine mirror of relationship. We will explore the energetic and metaphysical reasons for being in relationship to people around us. We'll discuss why we draw people, situations, and experiences into our lives and how this exchange of energy serves to grow and strengthen our soul force and the soul force of others. This will lead to a rigorous analysis of who we are at home, with our families, with friends, in romance, and in the workplace. We will also discuss and begin to work with spiritual guidance, from animal guides, spirit guides, and helpful healing spirits like the Council of Masters, who I mentioned in the opening of *Awakening Soul Force*. Should you decide to join me again, this journey will continue to deepen our spiritual practice and open the spiritual lens through which we view and experience our lives. There's no rush, though.

JEFF BOMBERGER

All in divine timing. Now go on—it's time for us to be on our way and get to intimately know soul force for ourselves.

PLEDGE OF PEACE, LOVE, AND UNITY

The wisdom of soul force calls us to express the higher spiritual ideals of peace, love, and unity through our lived humanity: Give life to love. Give birth to peace. Give rise to heaven on Earth by honoring our unified human experience. We can create a free world—a world free from suffering, free from guilt, free from shame, free from fear, and free from violence—if we pledge our lives to practicing peace, love, and unity. Consider taking the following pledge of peace, love, and unity, and join the soul-force movement by adding your name to the list of fellow seekers who have made the same pledge at www.thesoulforce.com.

I hereby pledge to uphold the following intentions to the best of my abilities in an effort to build a better world for myself, my family, my community, and generations to come.

JEFF BOMBERGER

PLEDGE OF PEACE, LOVE, AND UNITY

1. I pledge to honor peace, love, and unity in thought, word, and deed.
2. I pledge to be a model of peace, love, and unity in all aspects of my life, to the best of my abilities.
3. I pledge to love my neighbors, including my enemies, as my family.
4. I pledge to not guilt or shame others but instead to seek to understand and reconcile differences through open, constructive dialogue.
5. I pledge to not judge others but instead to love and support our mutual growth toward peace, love, and unity.
6. I pledge to honor the truth that we are all connected through our shared humanity.
7. I pledge to honor our shared basic human rights and justice.
8. I pledge to lovingly—but firmly—refuse to cooperate with hate, abuse, violence, and forces that seek to divide all people and our sacred human union.
9. I pledge to take the steps I can to deconstruct and eradicate poverty, racism, and violence in all forms by living a life of service and elevating human dignity in whatever way I can.
10. I pledge to work toward building an inclusive, beloved, and sacred community for all.

Thank you for joining me on this journey and entertaining my thoughts, experiences, and stories.

*I hope our paths will cross again soon.
Until then, onward and inward into the soul force!*

JOIN THE SOUL FORCE

Visit www.thesoulforce.com for soul-stimulating digital content, guided meditation downloads, and other information created to inspire us on our journey with soul force!

www.ingramcontent.com/pod-product-compliance
Lightning Source LLC
Chambersburg PA
CBHW071300110526
44591CB00010B/730